Table of Contents

Preface

Thank you for purchasing this book, which is the third and final book in the Preparing for the Unexpected series. This book is arguably the most important book in the series, as it delves into a topic that rarely receives attention—post-disaster recovery. While much attention is placed on preparedness and planning, little to no attention is dedicated to thinking about how to rebuild, recover, and reopen after an emergency or disaster.

As this book details, recovering from an emergency or disaster is a Herculean task—and certainly one that should not be underestimated. To help put things into perspective, imagine being asked to make some of the most consequential decisions of your life when you don't even know where you, or your family, will be sleeping at night. The chaos, stress, anxiety, and depression that accompany these situations are indeed real and should be accounted for when planning your response. As with other aspects of preparedness, more advanced planning often leads to more successful outcomes.

From a personal perspective, this book means a lot to me. When I first agreed to write this book, I was supporting the US Virgin Islands (USVI) and Puerto Rico Departments of Health in their post-hurricane recovery and rebuilding efforts. You may recall that in September 2017 the Caribbean was hit by two powerful hurricanes, Irma and Maria. Both were Category 5, and they hit less than two weeks apart, causing widespread damage, destruction, and suffering. Through our work, we were interfacing directly with early childhood programs. We helped them to better understand their needs and the impact the hurricanes had on their programs and on the children and families that they serve. Importantly, we also worked to help develop tools and resources to assist with the recovery from the next hurricane or disaster, with an eye toward minimizing its impact.

While the Caribbean certainly had its challenges, including supply shortages, worker shortages, the eviction of the Puerto Rican government, and even earthquakes in Puerto Rico, no one could have imagined the challenges that the next few years would bring.

The publication of this book has been delayed on three different occasions due to unique situations and circumstances. First, the emergence of COVID-19 and the ensuing pandemic caused a delay. Second, the book was put on hold as my wife and I celebrated the birth of our first child, Rachel Stella Roszak. Her birth gave new meaning and emphasis to the important, daily work of early childhood professionals. Rachel's arrival also re-emphasized the importance of ensuring that early childhood professionals are well versed and prepared to handle these very challenging issues.

Certainly, COVID-19 and the birth of our first child were more than enough to keep us busy. However, the world works in mysterious ways. The book was delayed for a third time when my family lived through a horrific tornado that struck our community, leaving eighty-six homes damaged or destroyed, another fifty-six condemned, and three of our neighbors dead. This terrible event occurred around midnight on a random February night when Rachel had just turned three weeks old. To first-time parents, this unexpected disaster certainly added a tremendous amount of additional complexity to our lives. I wish that none of my readers have a similar personal experience. Yet, ironically, our personal exposure to natural disaster has made the content of this book more informed and detailed than I previously would have thought possible.

Shortly after the tornado impacted our family, I felt severely overwhelmed and depressed. I felt hopeless. The COVID-19 pandemic had ruined a lot of things—birthday parties, weddings, graduations—and taken hundreds of thousands of lives. There was not much we could plan for, as events routinely got canceled or indefinitely postponed. However, the birth of our first child was something that we could plan for—and my wife and I did everything possible to create the happiest home for her that we could. Her arrival offered an outlet for us to pour our positive energy into. Knowing that the COVID-19 pandemic had upended the world, at least we were certain that our home would be a safe and loving environment for our newest family member.

Sadly, all that was changed in just a few short minutes. The power of the tornado left a path of destruction and despair that is not easy to describe. Seeing everything you had planned for taken away in just a few minutes was heartbreaking. In fact, it was really beyond heartbreaking—it was a feeling of utter *helplessness.*

One day everything was just going wrong. I was fighting with contractors, insurance companies, suppliers—just doing a ton of things that I never imagined I would be doing on our maternity/paternity leave. I had also come to the realization that our baby would never get to sleep in the nursery that my wife and I had spent so much time, attention, and effort on making perfect. It was a gut-punch.

I paused for a moment and reflected that we would never get this time back. Never again would we be first-time parents welcoming our newest family member to our lives. Here I was, totally unfocused on her—instead I was focused on all the day-to-day things that post-disaster life brings. I felt a sense of loss not just on Rachel's behalf but an overall loss of purpose that really made me really question whether or not my priorities were in order—and if, at three weeks in, I was failing as a father.

Later that day, I received an email from Iran Rodriguez, a friend and colleague. In typical Iran style, it didn't say much, but what it did say changed my day. The subject line was simple: "Keep this message in your mind." When I opened the email, I saw a picture of a plaque with this caption: "To the world you are a dad. To our family you are the world." That message from Iran was all the reminder I needed to get refocused and reenergized. I still have that email in my inbox, marked as unread, and from time to time I refer back to it. No matter the situation, it serves as an important reminder to keep things in perspective.

Throughout this book, I speak from my twenty-plus years in emergency preparedness and disaster response, including lessons learned during my time in the Caribbean after hurricanes Irma and Maria. And, just as the voices of others who have lived through trying times can teach us a lot, I can now also include personal insights and reflections from our own ten-month post-tornado rebuilding process. We have developed a special website, https://www.childhoodpreparedness.org/recovery, which provides tools, resources, and videos of early childhood professionals who have lived through emergencies and disasters.

My heartfelt appreciation to those who have made this book possible and those who have supported me, my family, and my business, the Institute for Childhood Preparedness, during these very difficult times. Special thanks to my wife, Dr. Sara Roszak, for her always-present love and overabundant support; my father, Ronald Roszak, for his continued dedication to keeping children safe; Dr. Demi Woods, who provided countless hours of support and research in support of this publication; and Dr. Zakary Woods, for his contributions and editing eagle eye. I also need to acknowledge Mr. Iran Rodriguez. I have had the privilege of working side by side with Iran on disaster preparedness and recovery issues for more than five years. His compassion, spirit, and, most importantly, his sense of humor have served as an inspiration and provided much-needed comic relief during stressful situations.

I sincerely hope this book helps you become better prepared; and if you are ever in the unfortunate position of having to rebuild and recover, I hope you keep Iran's simple message in mind: to your family you are the world.

Introduction

In 2017, hurricanes Maria and Irma caused considerable damage to the US Virgin Islands (USVI) and Puerto Rico. As Category 5 storms, they caused widespread destruction and disruption and the deaths of more than 3,000 people. In the aftermath of these storms, many early childhood programs were damaged and closed. Delays in funding, supplies, and ready access to professional services caused extended closure of many early childhood sites.

To better understand the impact of these hurricanes in the Caribbean, the Institute for Childhood Preparedness, together with the National Environmental Health Association, the Region II Head Start Association, the Puerto Rico Department of Health, and the US Virgin Islands Department of Health, conducted a series of meetings in Puerto Rico and the USVI. This work was funded by the US government through the Agency for Toxic Substances and Disease Registry (ATSDR). This was the first and only known attempt to tell the story of those entrusted to protect the health and well-being of children as they recover from disaster.

In addition to collecting data to better understand the hurricanes' impacts, participants in the meetings also reached a consensus that additional information and resources could aid the timely reopening of early childhood programs. Through discussions with the US Department of Health and Human Services' Administration for Children and Families, it became clear that no quick, easy-to-use method existed to assess the condition of early childhood programs after a disaster.

Recognizing the importance of reopening these programs in a timely manner, along with the realization that many are overwhelmed after a disaster, the goal was simple: develop an easy-to-use and easy-to-understand tool to help identify hazards that may impede reopening after a disaster. Our charge was to develop this resource and ensure that it met the needs of the early childhood community.

We knew from past disasters that children, older adults, people with disabilities, and those living in poverty are the most vulnerable to experiencing adverse effects after a disaster. An effort by the Instituto Desarrollo Juventud (Cox Marrero et al., 2018a) helped quantify some of the impacts of Hurricane Maria on families in Puerto Rico with children eighteen years and younger. Not surprisingly, their efforts found that low-income families (with annual incomes less than $15,000) fared much worse when compared to families with incomes greater than $15,000. This was true across all categories, including food security, utilities, employment, transportation, and medical services.

The report also highlighted the migration that occurs after disasters and found that nearly a third of families stated it was probable or very probable that they would migrate as a result of the hurricanes. As we have discussed, this is a very important consideration for early childhood programs: you may rebuild and finally reopen your doors only to find that many of your clients have moved away.

Our on-the-ground outreach efforts yielded some important results and uncovered some interesting findings. We held four regional meetings in Puerto Rico and the USVI with early childhood professionals. For example, in Puerto Rico the early childhood professionals who participated in these meetings served a combined total of more than 25,000 children and had more than six hundred years of collective experience working in the early childhood profession. In Puerto Rico, 85 percent of early childhood providers in attendance reported damage to their programs. They also reported that their programs were closed for an average of six weeks.

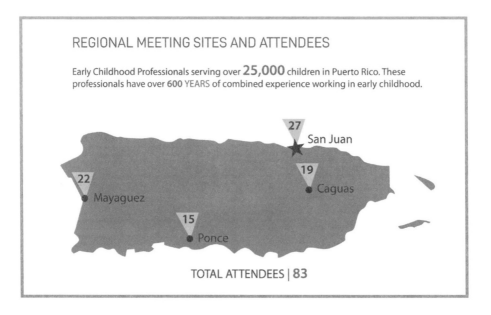

REGIONAL MEETING SITES AND ATTENDEES

Early Childhood Professionals serving over **25,000** children in Puerto Rico. These professionals have over **600 YEARS** of combined experience working in early childhood.

27 San Juan

22 Mayaguez

19 Caguas

15 Ponce

TOTAL ATTENDEES | 83

Across both Puerto Rico and the USVI, early childhood programs faced similar barriers that prevented the timely reopening of programs: lack of electricity, water, and food; mudslides; mold; and debris. Almost two years later, early childhood professionals and children were still experiencing the negative impacts of these hurricanes.

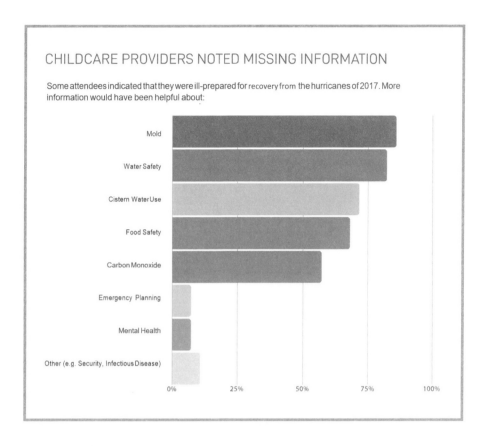

CHILDCARE PROVIDERS NOTED MISSING INFORMATION

Some attendees indicated that they were ill-prepared for recovery from the hurricanes of 2017. More information would have been helpful about:

Key takeaways from our engagements include the following:

- To stay in operation and meet community needs, 21 percent had to change locations.
- Fifty-four percent had to change their hours.
- On average, seventy-two fewer children were enrolled in the child-care programs.
- When providers could finally reopen, many of the children had left because reopening took so long.
- Providers reported mold; flooding; damage to roofs, fences, windows, doors, air conditioning, and outdoor equipment; and lack of electricity, which some providers still struggle with today.
- Barriers noted included lack of food and resources, inaccessible facilities, mudslides, debris removal, mold, and contaminated water.

How This Book Is Organized

This is the third book in the Preparing for the Unexpected Series. The first book, *Preschool Preparedness for an Active Shooter*, focuses on increasing the safety and security of your facility. The second book, *Preschool Preparedness for an Emergency*, focuses on planning for an emergency and creating procedures for use during an emergency. This book covers the aftermath of the emergency. It is designed to walk you through the various phases of disaster recovery. Sadly, for many, disaster recovery is often an afterthought, and the complexities of recovering and rebuilding are left to be learned in the middle of a crisis. That is hardly an ideal approach. If you have read my other books or have attended one of my training sessions, you know one of my favorite slogans is "Practice makes prepared." This is especially true in the post-disaster recovery world.

There are so many actors involved in disaster recovery and so many unique considerations to take into account, it can be—and will be—overwhelming. The more you learn about these topics ahead of time, the better and faster your recovery process will be. This book is designed to get you up to speed on the various elements of disaster recovery. We explore the nuances of insurance and define key insurance terms. We discuss mental-health considerations and the importance of taking proactive measures to practice self-care. We discuss common injuries that occur in the post-disaster environment. We explore working with insurance and selecting contractors to repair and remediate damage. Finally, we discuss reopening the early childhood program in a manner that is as safe as possible. I purposefully have included numerous stories, first-hand accounts, and factual information to help provide real-world context to the themes and issues that are discussed here. In addition to what you see in the following pages, we have also developed a website (https://www.childhoodpreparedness.org/recovery) where you can find resources, tools, and videos from early childhood professionals who have lived through real-world emergencies.

Considering Disaster Management

Disaster management follows a cycle. At the most basic level, the disaster-management cycle consists of four basic parts. This book focuses on one of the most important but often neglected parts—recovery. Why does recovery tend to be neglected? Many reasons exist, but the primary reason is that we often live under the impression that "It will never happen here." Our goal is to spend as little time in the recovery portion of the cycle as possible.

When we are in recovery, by definition, life is not normal. Returning to normal operations helps everyone—it is better for our business, better for our mental health, and better for the community that we serve.

- **Preparation** involves the development and testing of emergency-action plans. Preparedness is a continuing commitment, which requires monetary investment. Organizations should not view preparedness as being done once the plan is written. Instead, they should test the plan, reevaluating whether the plan needs revisions. Other examples include stockpiling food and water.

- **Response** occurs when an emergency or disaster begins. It requires us to take action to protect lives and property. During a response, our investments in planning and training are put to the test. This is game day or "go time." Organizations that have invested in their mitigation and preparedness efforts will have responses that are effective and efficient. Such planning limits damage and loss of life and allows us to move past the emergency in a more expeditious manner.

1

- **Recovery** comes after the immediate threat to life and property has ended and involves picking up the pieces and attempting to return to normal. Recovery can be a long road—and for some communities, it may take years to fully recover. Recovery often contains short- and long-term efforts. For example, establishing a shelter to meet the needs of displaced individuals is a short-term recovery goal; whereas, rebuilding homes destroyed by the disaster is a long-term recovery goal. Each recovery effort seeks to bring stability to the impacted community.

- **Mitigation** efforts seek to reduce potential harm or loss from emergencies or disasters. Mitigation activities are completed before a response and involve conducting activities to lower risk. For instance, a city may enact building codes to reduce the impact of high winds or floods on buildings. By enacting these codes, the city is seeking to reduce the potential losses that may be incurred from a disaster. Another example is purchasing insurance.

The disaster-management cycle is especially important for small businesses, which often feel the tangible impact of a disaster just as a family would. Small businesses account for 99 percent of all companies and employ 50 percent of all private-sector employees (US Department of Homeland Security, Earthquake Country Alliance, and Federal Alliance for Safe Homes, n.d.). Communities across the United States depend on small businesses for everyday needs, including for early child care and education.

Effects on Early Childhood Programs

Many early childhood programs are small businesses. According to the Committee for Economic Development of The Conference Board (CED), 768,521 child-care establishments were operating in the country in 2019, with approximately 90 percent being classified as family child-care programs or one-person operations (CED, 2019; Stevens, 2017). While certainly large in quantity, when compared to child-care centers, family child-care providers generated approximately 25 percent of total revenue for the entire early childhood sector. While workforce numbers are difficult to quantify, several groups estimate at least 12 million children under the age of six are in a child-care arrangement.

Sadly, the US Federal Emergency Management Agency (FEMA) estimates that between 40 and 60 percent of small businesses do not reopen after a disaster. Resuming operations as soon as possible is vital, as there is a direct correlation between the time it takes to reopen and the likelihood of continued operations. Doing so allows you to resume your cash flow, and importantly, let your customers know you are back open. Being unable to reopen after an emergency can have dire consequences. Nearly 90 percent of small businesses that do not reopen within **five days** of a disaster will fail within a year (FEMA and Federal Alliance for Safe Homes, n.d.a). Additionally, nearly 75 percent of businesses without emergency preparedness and continuity planning will fail within three years of a disaster (FEMA and Federal Alliance for Safe Homes, n.d.b). While this is tragic for any one business, the loss of an early childhood program in a community can be downright disastrous.

These statistics are important and help paint a clear picture for policymakers and professional emergency-management organizations. These facts and figures show the importance of child care as a business. We also need to consider the impact that a lack of child-care services has on a community.

While we all face the possibility of experiencing disasters, only 49 percent of child-care administrators in both residential and child-care centers report being able to properly care for children during and after disasters. Of those, 37 percent of administrators in child-care centers report being able to provide care to children for longer than twenty-four hours during and after an emergency (Leser, Looper-Coats, and Roszak, 2019).

If child care is not available, parents are unable to work. In communities suffering from the disaster, rebuilding and recovery efforts can be delayed without adequate child care. Little research has been done about the economic impacts of post-disaster closure of early childhood programs. However, a study looking at typical breakdowns in child care—children being sick, child-care programs temporarily closing, issues with transportation, and other routine events—found that lack of access to child care costs $8.3 billion in lost wages each year (Glynn and Corley, 2016). One can only speculate that this figure would severely increase in the event of a prolonged absence of early childhood programs within a community.

Furthermore, vulnerable populations, such as children, older adults, people with disabilities, and those living in poverty, are the most likely to experiencing adverse effects in a post-disaster environment. This is important as early childhood programs begin to think about the clients that they serve and the staff that they employ. Families that were barely making it prior to the emergency or disaster will likely need assistance in the post-disaster environment. This is a special consideration that must be taken into account. Consider how you may best help these clients, such as supporting them through cash donations, tangible goods (food, water, or clothing), tuition relief, or even transportation. Depending on the clientele you serve, this could include a substantial portion of your clients, especially if your program traditionally serves families below the poverty thresholds (such as Head Start programs).

The severe damage suffered by Puerto Rico after Hurricane Maria in 2017 helps to provide a snapshot. After the hurricane, 99.7 percent of families with children younger than the age of eighteen were without electricity for an average of 103 days, and 85 percent of such families lost water service for an average of 55 days. A report by Instituto Desarrollo Juventud (2018) examined the impacts of Hurricane Maria on a representative sample of families with children eighteen years and younger in Puerto Rico. Findings consistently showed that poorer families (with incomes less than $15,000) fared much worse from the aftermath of the hurricane compared to families with higher incomes. These outcomes were seen in all categories (food security, utilities, employment, transportation, medical services). In this study, nearly a third of families reported that it was probable or very probable that they would migrate because of the hurricane.

The Puerto Rican experience was not unique: findings in the USVI after Hurricane Irma, which hit both the USVI and Puerto Rico two weeks before Maria, were similar. The USVI Kids Count report found that the poverty levels for families in the USVI with children increased from 27 percent to 32 percent, and more households received Supplemental Nutrition Assistance Program (SNAP) benefits in September 2018 than during the two years prior to the hurricanes. Similarly, in the 2016–2017 school year, only fifteen families received emergency or crisis intervention that provided essential needs such as food, clothing, and shelter; that number increased to 300 families that received those services in the 2017–2018 school year, after the hurricanes (Community Foundation of the Virgin Islands, 2018; Michael et al., 2019).

The Head Start program administered by the USVI Department of Human Services in Puerto Rico is the most comprehensive childhood program in the territory. Head Start can provide services to 894 eligible children each year in its fifteen centers with forty-five classrooms across the three main islands of St. Croix, St. John, and St. Thomas. Due to damage from Hurricanes Irma and Maria, classrooms had to be consolidated. The Head Start centers in St. John and St. Thomas remain closed, as well as the two centers in St. Croix. Many more centers were less seriously damaged and able to reopen, but still operate with unrepaired damages.

Enrollment at Head Start across the territory decreased more than 50 percent from the beginning of the school year to the end. For private child care (not to be confused with Head Start), the USVI Department of Human Services reported that twenty-seven child-care centers in the St. Thomas–St. John district closed, along with twelve centers on St. Croix. The territory's private child-care centers lost more than half their capacity in available space and number of children enrolled due to damage to the facilities and families moving off the islands.

Migration is a phenomenon that occurs after every disaster. For example, massive migration was seen after Hurricane Katrina struck the Gulf Coast of the United States in 2005. In fact, all fifty states, the District of Columbia, and Puerto Rico received families affected by the hurricane's devastation (Ericson, Tse, and Wilgoren, 2005). More recently, USVI and Puerto Rico experienced this phenomenon as well.

The diaspora of families and children away from the impacted area is something that early childhood programs should take into account when developing their recovery plans. Staying in close contact with your clients and families during recovery is an important consideration and can help you better understand their situations and future child-care needs. Sadly, as the above information illustrates, some early childhood programs reopened only to find that a substantial portion of their families had moved away. This certainly has an impact on program operations and funding.

2

Insurance Basics

According to the Insurance Information Institute (III), one out of every fifteen US homeowners files a claim on their homeowners insurance each year. This astonishing number reinforces the need to be familiar with your business or home insurance policy in advance of any damaging event. The III also reports that the average home insurance claim is for $16,000 and the average home insurance premium is $1,173 per year (III, 2022).

Insurance policies can be confusing, especially because they may have different levels of out-of-pocket expenses for different causes or claims. In the following pages we will discuss different types of policies and deductibles. Some of these disparities are heavily influenced by what region or state you live in. Due to this geographic variance and to the fact that the insurance industry is constantly evolving, it is important to check with your insurance carrier to be sure you have the latest information regarding policies and deductibles. We strongly recommend also checking with your insurance carrier to help determine which insurance is recommended for your area and your particular situation.

Let's start with the basics. An insurance *deductible* is the amount the insured pays in the event of damage or a loss. Overall, it is a means for a client to share in the initial cost of a claim and defines the financial line between what repairs the insured covers versus those that the insurance company is responsible for. A deductible also provides a monetary incentive to properly maintain and protect your property from damage. Thus, the higher the deductible, the lower your insurance premiums. Conversely, a lower deductible typically means a higher premium.

Deductibles can be exceptionally confusing to understand, so here's a deeper look into how they work. Not every deductible is created equal. In some cases, special deductibles (or specific-peril deductibles) are applied separately for a higher dollar amount than the standard deductible. For example, if you have a $1,000 deductible for fire, theft, and all other perils, and you live on the coast, your deductible for windstorm and hail losses may be an additional $2,000 or higher.

Rather than dollar amounts, however, deductibles are sometimes expressed as a percentage of the coverage amount on your property. So, a wind deductible of

1 percent on a $300,000 property is $3,000, and a wind deductible of 2 percent would be $6,000. But a 5-percent wind deductible on a $700,000 property is $35,000! In coastal Massachusetts counties, wind deductibles of 1 percent, 2 percent, and 5 percent are the most common, especially for properties within a mile of the coast.

These deductibles are part of an effort by the insurance industry to limit their storm losses by having the insured share more of the repair costs. Property owners can take steps to protect their property when they are especially vulnerable to wind damage. After all, if you have a 5-percent deductible on a $500,000 property, you essentially have a $25,000 reason to consider investing in storm shutters, a generator, the highest quality shingles, fewer trees in the yard, and other protections for your property.

Standard Insurance Deductible

Insurance policies will list a standard insurance deductible, often termed the "All Other Perils" (AOP) deductible. The most common AOP deductibles are usually flat dollar amounts, such as $1,000, $2,500, and $5,000, although significantly larger ones are available for high-value properties or high-risk environments (sometimes this can apply to early childhood settings, depending on the size of the program). So, for example, an AOP deductible of $1,000 means that the insured will cover $1,000 worth of repairs, and insurance will cover the repairs beyond $1,000, up to a specified value.

The AOP deductible applies to covered damages to your property due to things such as lightning, fire, hail, vandalism, and theft, to name a few, and it applies for each occurrence. Let's say you have a theft claim in March, a hail claim in July, and a lightning claim in August. Each of these claims will be subject to the full amount of the deductible that's been set; thus for these three events, you would need to pay $1,000 x 3 = $3,000 out of pocket to meet your deductible.

If your insurance offers you a wind deductible, it normally will appear on the "Declarations" page of your insurance policy, which is often the very first page. Different insurance companies use different metrics for these specific-peril deductibles. The three most common approaches are the following:

- Wind-related deductibles (the broadest)
- Named-storm deductibles (common)
- Hurricane deductibles (less common)

Wind-Related Deductibles

Many policies stipulate a separate deductible for damage caused by wind. These deductibles are higher than the standard AOP deductible. As wind is the most common insurance claim, insurance companies handle wind damage with extreme caution. It is imperative to understand your policy and the specific deductibles caused by various factors. Common wind-related deductibles include wind, hail, named storms, and hurricanes.

WIND

If your property is located near the coast or in an area where damaging winds are a common threat, your policy will likely state a separate, higher deductible for this peril. Wind deductibles can be a specific amount, such as $10,000, or can be expressed as a percentage of the property coverage, such as 2 percent. To calculate the amount of a percentage deductible, take the insured amount of the property and multiply it by the deductible. For example, if you insure your property for $200,000 and your wind deductible is 2 percent, you are responsible for out-of-pocket costs of $4,000 ($200,000 x 0.02 = $4,000). Wind deductibles vary between 1 percent and 10 percent—unless your policy sets a specific amount.

Windstorm deductibles are the most inclusive of the deductibles offered, meaning they apply to most claims or whenever damage is caused by wind. Such claims include not only hurricanes and other tropical storms but also winter nor'easters and summer thunderstorms. Any kind of wind damage will prompt this higher exposure to the owner.

WIND AND/OR HAIL

Instead of a simple wind deductible, certain policies stipulate a separate deductible for damage due to wind or hail. Note that this kind of deductible is not as advantageous, as it applies when damage is caused by wind *and* hail, but not just wind alone.

Damage caused by wind, wind-driven rain or hail, or "all other perils" is separate from damage caused by a named hurricane. The deductible for this type of damage also may be set at a flat dollar amount of $500 or $1,000, although some carriers use a percentage amount for properties with coastal exposure (which means higher risk). If your property experiences damage from both a named hurricane and an unnamed windstorm in the same season, you will be responsible for both deductibles.

NAMED STORM

If your policy specifies a named-storm deductible, this deductible applies if the storm that causes the damage is numbered or named by the US National Weather Service (NWS), the US National Hurricane Center, or the US National Oceanic and Atmospheric Administration (NOAA). For example, Hurricane Irene and Tropical Storm David are named storms that would be included under a named-storm deductible. Unlike wind/hail, a named-storm deductible provides better coverage

than a wind deductible because it applies only for larger, named-storm events. Having named-storm coverage is a priority if you are in a coastal area where your property may be impacted by tropical storms.

To illustrate, the notorious "no-name" storm of March 1993 struck Florida and twenty-one other US states and caused $2 billion in damages (NWS, n.d.a). In Florida, the storm caused storm surges of up to 12 feet, winds in excess of 90 miles per hour, and tornadoes—effects similar to those of a hurricane. In Alabama, Georgia, and up the East Coast to Maine, the blizzard dumped snow, toppled trees, and knocked out power. Damage from that storm would not have been subject to a higher named-storm deductible but would have been under a wind deductible. The regular, smaller AOP deductible would have been used for any damage caused by the no-name storm under a named-storm deductible. But damage from Hurricane Irene, Hurricane Sandy, or other named storms would have invoked the wind and/or named-storm deductible.

HURRICANE

A hurricane deductible is one of the best wind-related deductibles because it applies only when a property is damaged by a hurricane. Most policies require the storm be categorized as a hurricane by the NWS or US National Hurricane Center. In Florida, the application of hurricane deductibles is triggered by wind-storm losses resulting only from a hurricane declared by the NWS. The hurricane deductible applies only once during each hurricane season, regardless of the number of hurricanes that season.

A hurricane deductible may be calculated in either one of two ways:

- **Percentage amount:** This type of deductible is calculated according to the value of the insured property and can be anywhere from 2 percent to 10 percent, although 2 percent is the most commonly used figure.
- **Flat dollar amount:** This type of deductible is typically $500 or $1,000. It's advisable to set aside this amount prior to hurricane season in case of damage to your property.

The insured can choose a higher premium with a lower or fixed dollar amount hurricane deductible or can select a lower premium with a higher percentage-based deductible. The hurricane deductible would apply to claims for damage that occurred from the time a hurricane watch or warning was issued until up to seventy-two hours after such a watch or warning ended, as well as anytime hurricane conditions exist anywhere in the state.

Hurricane Sandy is a good example of the distinction between named-storm and hurricane deductibles. On October 29, 2012, when Sandy made landfall in New Jersey, it was downgraded from a Category 1 hurricane to a tropical storm (NWS, n.d.b). Thus, the lower AOP deductible applied to those insured with a hurricane deductible. Hurricane deductibles have become less common due to the potential for political interference after the fact, as was evident with Sandy. Some suggested that the downgrade of Hurricane Sandy was precisely announced to shield insured property owners from the hurricane deductible—a boon for consumers with that one event. But insurance carriers quantify risk precisely, and after-the-fact interference prompted changes for the next event. Thus, what were once called *hurricane* deductibles have morphed into *named-storm* deductibles in most coastal regions. After Hurricane Andrew in 1992, which caused an estimated $26.5 billion in damage in the United States (National Hurricane Center and Central Pacific Hurricane Center, n.d.), insurers realized that losses from hurricanes could be much higher than they had previously thought. Hurricane Katrina, in 2005, which cost insurers more than $41 billion at the time, confirmed their fears (Hartwig and Wilkinson, 2010). After these extraordinary losses, reinsurance companies—insurers that share the cost of claims with primary companies, such as homeowners' insurers—decided that they could not assume so much risk and that primary companies must reduce their potential losses.

During the Atlantic hurricane season, which lasts from June to November, every coastal state from Florida to Maine can potentially be hit by a storm. Increasing development along the coastal areas of these states has put more and more properties at risk of severe windstorm damage. To limit their exposure to catastrophic losses from natural disasters, insurers in these states sell insurance policies with percentage deductibles instead of the traditional dollar deductibles, which are used for other types of losses such as fire damage and theft.

To some degree, depending on the state, insurance companies determine the level of the hurricane, windstorm, or wind/hail deductible and where it should apply. Florida is an exception; state law dictates these variables. Insurers' hurricane deductible plans must be reviewed by each state's insurance department, where they may be subject to various regulations and laws.

Nineteen states and the District of Columbia have hurricane deductibles: Alabama, Connecticut, Delaware, Florida, Georgia, Hawaii, Louisiana, Maine, Maryland, Massachusetts, Mississippi, New Jersey, New York, North Carolina, Pennsylvania, Rhode Island, South Carolina, Texas, Virginia, and Washington, DC (National Association of Insurance Commissioners, 2021).

Flood Deductibles

According to the National Oceanic and Atmospheric Administration (NOAA)'s National Severe Storms Laboratory (NSSL), floods are the most common and most widespread natural disasters to occur. All fifty states and each US territory is at risk for flooding. In fact, floods kill more people in the United States each year than tornadoes, lightning, or hurricanes (NOAA NSSL, n.d.).

In August 2021, a Cobb County, Georgia, early childhood facility was impacted by swift moving floodwaters. The water rose so quickly and so high that emergency services had to be called to help evacuate the facility. In total, twenty-seven children and four adults were evacuated by local emergency responders (Morgan, 2021). (Note: you can see the videos from this incident at https://www.childhoodpreparedness.org/recovery).

The first step in determining your risk for flooding is to become familiar with your local area. FEMA offers a free, online flood map website that you can use to determine if your early childhood facility or family home is located in an area at risk for flooding. Use the FEMA website (https://msc.fema.gov/portal/home) to locate flood maps for your community.

Damage caused by flooding is a separate deductible that applies under a flood-insurance policy. Again, a flat dollar amount or a percentage amount may apply, and the deductible for the property itself will be different from the deductible for personal belongings. Overall, setting aside money for deductibles in a savings account can help you prepare for an upcoming storm season, as can taking steps to protect your property from hurricane or flooding damage.

While no one plans for their property to get damaged, the reality is that storm damage can and does happen. Clearly a reliable and inclusive insurance policy is a wise investment. However, even if your insurance covers the cost of replacing some or all of your damaged property, you still would experience the inconvenience of fixing whatever went wrong.

Flooding can happen due to heavy rain, stalled weather fronts, and even storm surges caused by hurricanes. In 2017, Hurricane Irma, a Category 5 storm, struck the Caribbean and then moved north to impact the Florida Keys and the eastern side of Florida. At https://www.childhoodpreparedness.org/recovery, you can view the stories of three early childhood programs affected by these storms. Banana Cabana, a child care in the Florida Keys, was hit particularly hard. Roxanne Rosado from Banana Cabana shares her insights on the challenges to rebuilding and reopening. Several hundred miles away, the Early Learning Coalition of St. Lucie County saw their offices flooded by the storm. In the interview, Tony Loupe, the executive director, takes time to walk through what was left of the child-care resource and referral agency, discusses how his agency assisted early childhood professionals, and explains the importance of business continuity plans. The last interview features St. James Christian Academy, a child-serving institution that was severely damaged by floodwaters. In fact, the flooding was so severe that the owner had to use a canoe to reach the facility. These three interviews provide unfiltered advice and suggestions from those who have lived through disasters.

Earthquake Insurance Coverage

Much like the other special situations we discuss in this chapter, earthquakes are not covered by standard homeowners' insurance. FEMA has noted that the United States is "underprepared for earthquakes" from an insurance standpoint.

As evidence, it points to the fact that 90 percent of earthquakes in the United States occur in California; however, only 10 percent of California residents have earthquake insurance (FEMA, 2021). There are various websites that show the risk of an earthquake in your area. This information can be used to help inform your decision about whether or not to purchase earthquake insurance. For example, the California Earthquake Authority (CEA), the country's largest provider of earthquake insurance, has a website that provides county-level information about the likelihood of a 7.0 or greater earthquake occurring, along with the number of active fault lines (CEA, 2022). Earthquake insurance can be complicated, so it is important to have a discussion with your insurance provider to understand exactly what is and is not covered by the policy. For example, if an earthquake causes a water pipe to burst in your home and your home subsequently receives water damage, it would likely be your regular homeowners' insurance that covers the damage. However, if the earthquake caused your building to collapse or destroyed personal property in your home, then that would likely be covered by the earthquake insurance (Grace, 2022).

There are also two common types of earthquake insurance: traditional and parametric. Traditional insurance protects you against "pure loss," which means the value of the items that are lost due to earthquake damage, such as a television falling off the wall and being destroyed. Parametric insurance is a newer type of earthquake insurance. This type uses different parameters to determine the cost of the damage, and payments are only provided if these parameters are satisfied. Generally, for earthquakes these parameters are often the magnitude of the actual earthquake itself. For example, if the parametric insurance only covers earthquakes of a magnitude 6.0 or higher, damage from a 5.0 earthquake would not be covered by this insurance (FEMA, 2021).

Common Insurance Claims

Without a doubt, insurance is a data-driven business. Establishing premiums and calculating losses invariably revolve around hard data from insurance claims. Fortunately, you can use some of this data to help make you better prepared and reduce the likelihood of damage to your property. According to The Hartford insurance company (Harbour, 2021), the seven most common claims are as follows:

1. Exterior wind damage
2. Non-natural event water damage
3. Weather-related water damage
4. Loss due to theft
5. Fire damage
6. Electrical fire
7. Slip and fall on your property

Yes, electrical fires are in their own category. Harbour states that they account for approximately 51,000 fires annually.

For some of these claims, taking simple steps can help reduce risk. Performing routine upkeep and maintenance on both the inside and outside of your property can go a long way. For the exterior of your property, this includes trimming trees, cutting back landscaping, and ensuring pathways are clear from weather elements and well maintained. When you receive notice that a storm is approaching, take proactive steps to secure outdoor objects, including children's toys and sunshades. Routinely make sure that all gutters are clear of debris, downspouts are clear, and water is properly draining away from your building.

Inside the property, routinely inspect water lines, drains, sinks, refrigerator ice-makers, washing machines, and toilets to make sure lines are not pinched, compromised, or leaking. Several products available on the market today can help monitor water leaks inside your building. Some of these send out audible alerts, and some even connect to the internet and can notify you on your smartphone. As always, be sure you have working smoke detectors and carbon-monoxide detectors present in your property.

Preventing fires is yet another area where a little bit of effort can go a long way. It is amazing that more than five hundred fires take place in early childhood programs in the United States each year (Campbell, 2017). We owe it to ourselves, and especially the children we are entrusted to care for, to make sure we are practicing good housekeeping techniques and minimizing our risk of fire. Avoid overloading outlets, limit the use of extension cords to temporary use, and routinely inspect cords and replace at the first sign of fraying or chewing damage by rodents. Luckily, most early childhood facilities get inspected regularly by the fire department or fire marshal. However, if your property hasn't recently been professionally inspected, it may be a good idea to contact a licensed professional and review your electrical wiring.

According to insurance data, about one in 325 insured homes have a theft claim each year (Harbour, 2021). Preventing thefts and violence should be a top priority—especially because we are working with children. Consider installing security cameras or even a security system. These cameras and systems can be found at very reasonable prices, and most allow for self-installation. Simple precautions such as replacing exterior light bulbs can also minimize the likelihood of theft or assaults.

As we have explored in this chapter, there is tremendous variation in the types of insurance offered. Knowing the different types of policies and their limitations is important. Likewise, taking proactive steps to help minimize damage or destruction to your property is strongly encouraged. The good news is that all of the above can be done at your own pace. When not faced with the immediacy of an emergency or disaster, we can approach these topics and tasks in a calm and organized fashion. Although some of this may not seem like glamorous work, it is vital that you fully understand what is and what is not covered by your policies. This knowledge will help set the stage for the following pages, where we will discuss more of the mechanics of working with insurance and contractors.

Beginning the Recovery Process

You have prepared your facility and your staff. Your property is insured. You have done as much as you can to be ready. Then, a disaster that you hoped wouldn't occur happens. In the aftermath of a disaster, so many issues arise that addressing them can become overwhelming. Especially during times of chaos and uncertainty, it is important to have built relationships in advance with people you can trust; earning and building trust is a process that takes time. Often after a disaster, relationships are formed quickly, and many require a leap of faith. It is important to understand the various roles and positions that people play in the recovery process. Unfortunately, not all people you come across during disaster recovery are forthright and honest. You need to look out for your best interests and not necessarily lean on others to do so. Equipping yourself with information and planning before a disaster will help you navigate the recovery period successfully. By understanding the various player roles and responsibilities, you can better determine who is your advocate and who may be your adversary. You will need to decide whom to trust and whom to hire, and you will need to enlist your insurance provider in helping you pay for repairs or rebuilding.

Answering some of these questions may depend on the scope and scale of your disaster, and to some degree, the location of the disaster. For incidents that have smaller minor damage, such as a burst pipe or a small kitchen fire, you may be able to hire your own contractors and fix the problem relatively easily. However, for incidents that cause greater damage or more complicated repairs, it may make sense to hire a company that specializes in recovery and restoration. Such a company would essentially serve as your general contractor and oversee the various experts that would be required to help you recover and rebuild.

Whether you choose to use a restoration company or form direct relationships with more specialized contractors, it is always important to vet these individuals ahead of time. Depending on the scope of the disaster, these entities may or may not have adequate resources to respond. In situations where multiple properties are damaged, companies may be overwhelmed and, quite frankly, understaffed.

They may not be able to handle the management and reconstruction process of multiple sites in different locations. The research and planning you do in advance of an emergency or disaster increases the likelihood of improved outcomes. Such planning would allow you to create a ready-made list of professionals and contractors whom you can call upon as needed.

Vetting and Choosing Restoration and Repair Companies

Spend some time researching plumbing, electrical, construction, and restoration companies. Good questions to consider include the following:

- Are they local? How long have they been in business in your area?
- Have other homeowners in your area hired them?
- Do they have references? If so, check them. What work was done? Did the service provider complete the work on time? Was the referring person satisfied with the work done?
- Are they licensed to do business in your area? Good resources are the Better Business Bureau or state attorney general's office.
- Have they worked with your insurance company before?
- Do they have an electronic system for quoting and submitting repair estimates?
- Do they have an office with administrative support?
- What is their payment policy? Do they want a substantial sum of money up front, or do they want to be paid at the end of the project? What types of payment do they take?
- Who will they use to get the supplies and materials for your job?
- What is the vetting process they use for hiring subcontractors?
- What work will they be personally doing, and what work do they plan to subcontract out? This could be plumbing, electrical, garage door or window repair, flooring, painting, and even cleaning.

Getting Needed Repairs after a Disaster

Living through a disaster is hard enough. Unfortunately, some individuals are faced with a second disaster when they experience scams or rip-off schemes from dishonest people or companies. Sadly, this is an all-too-common problem after disasters—so typical that the Federal Trade Commission and FEMA routinely issue consumer alerts to try to prevent disaster-stricken areas from being plagued by scams. There is even an annual campaign headed by the National Insurance Crime Bureau called "Contractor Fraud Awareness Week" that is designed to raise awareness of these issues.

The opportunities for fraudsters after a disaster are many. Some examples of schemes include trying to steal your identity, keeping your insurance settlement without completing the job, using inappropriate or inferior materials, manipulating the price, performing work that is not needed nor related to the disaster, and even performing low-quality work that is not up to code.

After the tornado devastated our community, I saw this play out at close quarters. A few of my neighbors even fell for the fraudsters—and signed contracts with them. After no work was performed for several months, it was obvious that they had been scammed. I can't adequately describe the feelings they expressed, knowing that they had been scammed, which delayed their repairs and ability to return to normal by about two months.

How to Avoid Fraudsters

In my opinion, individuals who commit these types of crimes are the lowest of the low. They prey on people who have just been through a horrible situation. These individuals often come into an area uninvited and begin targeting their victims. Luckily, you can employ several strategies to help prevent yourself from becoming a victim of fraud.

The following are a few tips that can help steer you in the right direction. In addition, the National Insurance Crime Bureau has developed a post-disaster contractor search checklist that walks through important considerations and decisions that should be made prior to hiring a contractor. The form can be found at https://www.childhoodpreparedness.org/recovery.

TRUST YOUR JUDGMENT

You probably have heard the saying that if something seems too good to be true, it often is. The same goes for these types of situations. Remember that an individual seeking to scam you will know all the right things to say and will look the part. They will usually show up uninvited, talk a mile a minute, and be pushy about having you sign something. A contractor's truck should have a company name, logo, phone number, and maybe even their license number. Be suspicious of individuals who show up in vehicles with no identifiers. These are all red flags.

An individual came to our home the morning after the tornado. He purposely waited until he saw me go to a neighbor's house to help with cleanup. He knocked on our door and told my wife that he was sent by the insurance company to begin determining what repairs were needed. He was very pushy and kept insisting that my wife sign a contract. Luckily, she declined, and I returned home while the man was still at the house. He continued to say he was sent by the insurance company and that other neighbors had already signed on to work with him. I simply asked him, "Oh, what insurance company?" When he looked at me dumbfounded and failed to provide an answer, I knew he was not legitimate. Similar instances were occurring throughout our community. The county sheriff posted law enforcement officers at all entrances to our community, and they checked each commercial vehicle to ensure they were licensed by the county to perform services. This helped eliminate the flow of fraudsters.

If you have spent some time researching companies before the disaster, you will have a better idea of reputable businesses in your area. If someone unknown to you does show up offering to help, ask questions such as: Are they local? Do they have references? Are they licensed to do business in your area? Be wary of out-of-state companies that suddenly show up after the disaster. Ideally, you want someone who is local and will be in your area long after the disaster.

DO NOT SIGN ANYTHING RIGHT AWAY

Any experienced professional who comes to help a disaster-stricken area should understand the emotion and severity of the situation. Be cautious of anyone trying to rush you into signing something. Also be careful of any forms that have a lot of blank spaces—those blanks can be fraudulently filled in with less-than-desirable terms after you've signed and the fraudster has left. It is perfectly legitimate, even essential, to take all offered materials, including the proposed contract, and read them over before making a decision. It is also a good idea to receive a quote or estimate from at least one other company before deciding to sign a contract.

BEWARE OF CONTRACTORS ASKING FOR UPFRONT PAYMENT

Money is always a sticky situation. This is a good topic to discuss with your insurance company. While it is not unusual to have a contractor request some payment upfront, it should never be a substantial amount. In my case, the only money I paid out of pocket was the cost to cover my homeowner's deductible.

Part of a written agreement should include the payment schedule. Most contractors either set specific milestones (for example, the roof is finished, the siding is replaced and painted, and so forth) or simply look for one lump-sum payment once all the work is complete. Remember that you will be getting a settlement from your insurance company. To avoid any out-of-pocket costs, you should understand how the insurance company will pay the claim. Some insurance companies prefer to pay smaller portions more frequently, while others issue a single payment once all the claims are submitted and the work has been completed.

There can also be variances in how the actual payment is handled. Some insurance companies provide the funds directly to the property owner. Others require the funds to be given to your mortgage holder. Still others have the checks made out to the contractor and the property owner, requiring both parties to endorse the check before it can be cashed. If someone is listed as an "other insured party" on your insurance policy, that person's or corporation's name will likely also be included on any settlement check. It is important to get clarity from your insurance carrier on just how the money will be paid out.

In any event, never pay a contractor in full or sign a completion certificate before the work is done to your satisfaction and you've confirmed it is in compliance with local and state codes. If you hold a mortgage on the property, the mortgage holder may even require an inspection before releasing funds.

CONFIRM ALL PERMITS AND LICENSES

We have building codes and permits for a reason—to ensure work is done properly! Having work inspected verifies that it meets codes, ordinances, and requirements. It is never okay for a contractor to skip or skirt the requirements for permitting and inspections. Situations in which a contractor cuts corners, especially related to completing work up to code, can create problems for property owners in the future. For instance, you wouldn't want to have an accident or unsafe situation due to poor work or have a problem selling the property years later because work was done illegally or improperly.

Similarly, your contractor should have a proper license issued by either the state or county for the work being performed. Most often, reputable companies include their contractor's license information on their business cards and vehicles and certainly on any written contracts. Remember, a *business* license is not the same as a *contractor's* license. There are a couple of things to keep in mind here. First, each state regulates businesses differently. It is important for you to be familiar with how your jurisdiction handles these issues. As a starting point, look to your jurisdiction's secretary of state or simply do an internet search for "business license" and your location. You will see that there are many different professions regulated by the government, everything from tattoo artists to hair stylists to pharmacy technicians to contractors. Let's try to unpack this a bit.

To legally conduct business in a state, the first thing a business needs is a business license. This is filed with the state and sets forth basic information about the business: who owns it, what type of ownership structure it has (such as a limited liability corporation, a nonprofit organization, etc.), and the names and addresses of those responsible for the business. Getting a business license is a relatively simple process, and for a few hundred dollars or less, a business can be established. Most states have a database where you can search businesses licenses. Each state is different, so again, an internet search may be the easiest way to quickly identify this information.

Individuals who repair or restore homes or businesses also must have a contractor's or trade license. There is one exception here, and that is for the handyman. A "handyman" is generally someone who completes small-scale jobs where the work is valued under a certain dollar amount; the amount varies by state. This could be someone who is simply installing a ceiling fan, swapping out a few light fixtures, installing a door—basically someone who is doing odd jobs and making small repairs to your home or business. Conversely, contractors usually specialize in one area, such as plumbing, electrical, gas, and so on and are often involved in large-scale projects. These contractors perform much more substantial work, such as replacing roofs, redoing or repairing structural issues with a building, running or repairing electrical wiring, and the like. To obtain their licensure, these contractors have proven their competency in their trade, have passed a general contractor exam, and have undergone a criminal background check. Again, this information can and does differ by state, so it is imperative that you visit the contractor's board website for your state to understand what is required of contractors in your area to obtain licensure and to determine how you can verify that a contractor's license is valid.

If you believe that you have fallen victim to a fraudulent company, contact your insurance company or local law-enforcement agency. You can also reach out to the National Insurance Crime Bureau at (800) 835-6422 or by submitting a form online at https://www.nicb.org/how-we-help/report-fraud.

Working with Your Insurance Company

Insurance companies vary widely throughout the United States. Recent years have seen a shift away from brick-and-mortar locations that allowed for an appointment and in-person visit with an agent. Now, much of the interaction with insurance companies happens online, which can be less customized and friendly than in-person interactions. While some online platforms can offer customers cost savings because they do not have facility costs, such as mortgage or rent, some drawbacks and disadvantages must still be anticipated.

The primary drawback is not having a relationship with a local agent who knows your local area. Also, you would not know who would be assigned as the adjuster for your case until after a disaster happens. It is important to note that the person who is your insurance agent may or may not be assigned as your insurance adjuster in the aftermath of a disaster; typically, agents are not assigned to be adjusters. An insurance *agent* is the individual who sells you insurance and serves as your first point of contact with your insurance company. An insurance *adjuster* is the individual who will investigate your claims and determine how much (if any) the insurance company should pay for the damages.

In some cases, an adjuster will come out to do an onsite, in-person inspection. In other situations, the adjuster may complete an online inspection or examine photos and/or video, such as those indicating property condition pre- and post-disaster, to verify and process your claim. Sometimes, insurance companies can get a tarnished reputation during disasters, and in some cases such a viewpoint has merit. However, by and large, insurance adjusters are fair people who are very well trained in disaster recovery. It should also be noted that many insurance companies have chosen to contract out their adjuster services. There may be cases in which you are working with an adjuster who is hired by your insurance company to help handle the claim on the company's behalf. This trend is becoming more common.

It is important to think about the insurance company as a vital relationship that should be cultivated for effective disaster recovery; it should not become an adversarial relationship.

One of the best ways to do this is to help make the insurer's job easier. Take photographs of your property before a disaster happens as well as after the disaster. Keep good records of your property maintenance, major purchases, and property improvements. Save receipts for any large purchases you make for your center. And be in routine communication with the insurance adjuster. As the policy holder, you should not wait for the insurance adjuster to contact you. Instead, foster a two-way relationship in which both parties can share updates and new information regarding the claim. It is not uncommon for adjusters to carry a heavy caseload. In some cases, they may be handling more than a hundred different claims. For best results with your adjuster, you should reference your claim number and other pertinent information about your case in each communication. Given the high caseload and shift toward handling some claims remotely, an insurance adjuster may not remember all the nuances about your particular situation.

**TIPS FOR WORKING WITH
YOUR INSURANCE ADJUSTER**

- Take photographs of your property *before* a disaster happens.

- Take photographs of the damage to your property *after* a disaster.

- Keep records of maintenance, major purchases, and improvements to your property.

- Save your receipts for purchases, such as an air-conditioning unit, a large climbing toy for the playground, a new stove in the kitchen, a curriculum and related materials for the preschool classrooms, and so on.

- Communicate regularly with your adjuster, referencing your claim number and any relevant information each time.

- Document each time you communicate with your adjuster. It is a good idea to send an email, so you have a written record, as phone conversations can easily be forgotten.

- As hard as it may be, do not take things personally. For you, this is extremely personal; for the insurance professionals, this is just another day doing their job.

Remember, during larger disasters it is common to have insurance adjusters be assigned to multiple cases. This is the reality, and it means that you will likely not get the personal attention that you may expect. It also means that you need to take proactive steps in communicating with the insurance company, so your claim is kept on their radar and does not get overlooked. Insurance adjusters come and go—in my community one of my neighbors had six different adjusters in the span of eight months—so it is vital to keep written records of what was discussed, what was agreed to, and agreed-upon timelines. That way when a new insurance adjuster takes over, everything is well documented and organized. Working with insurance can be stressful, especially when an insurance agent or adjuster is overloaded and is seemingly nonresponsive.

Without a doubt, this entire process can take a toll on your mental health. It is also likely that the children you normally serve will suffer some mental-health impacts, as their routines have been disrupted and their homes may have also suffered damage. In the next chapter, we explore mental-health considerations and discuss ways to incorporate self-help techniques into your disaster-recovery efforts.

4 Mental-Health Considerations

While physical damage to a home or a business is easy to see, the full scope and scale of mental trauma inflicted upon those experiencing a disaster is often overlooked. Unfortunately, the immediate focus is on the external, visible problems that require immediate assistance: tarping a roof, boarding up windows, and finding immediate shelter, to list a few. Long after the lights and sirens of the emergency-response vehicles have been turned off, the devastation and destruction of surrounding communities remain. Child-care professionals are in a unique situation because they not only help the children that they care for but also the parents that they serve and the community at large. In this chapter, we explore the issues surrounding mental and behavioral health in relation to trauma and disasters.

Understanding the Scope

The mental impacts of a disaster are a complex yet vital component to recovery and should be considered in your preparedness efforts. It is important that you understand and are able to recognize signs of mental struggles and that you familiarize yourself with local resources that may be of assistance.

The Centers for Disease Control and Prevention (CDC) reports that one in six US children ages two to eight years have a diagnosed mental, behavioral, or developmental disorder (2021a). The most common childhood mental-health disorders include attention deficit hyperactivity disorder (ADHD), behavior problems, anxiety, and depression. These facts and figures reflect our everyday society before any emergency or disaster. I think these are important to include because the data tells us that, as a starting point, we are already living in a society where these conditions are prevalent. As we have discussed elsewhere in the book, disasters and emergencies take pre-existing conditions and make them worse. Disasters compound previous problems, and those problems are likely to be even greater after a disaster. Consider the following:

- After the Oklahoma City bombing on April 19, 1995, alcohol consumption was 2.5 times greater than that of similarly situated communities.

- After a devastating tornado hit Joplin, Missouri, in 2001, alcohol use increased 80 percent.
- After the attacks on September 11, 2001, the use of anxiety medications increased by 19 percent in New York.
  (Community Partnership of the Ozarks, n.d.)

The World Health Organization has even stated that severe child abuse may increase after natural disasters. Sadly, affected communities have experienced this firsthand. In the six months after Hurricane Floyd caused widespread flooding in North Carolina, there was a fivefold increase in the number of children under age two who suffered from traumatic brain injury. Counties not impacted by the hurricane did not have the same traumatic results. In addition to the increase in alcohol use, Joplin, Missouri, also experienced a 40 percent increase in domestic violence (Community Partnership of the Ozarks, n.d.). Puerto Rico witnessed an uptick in suicides and depression after Hurricane Maria caused widespread damage to the island in 2017. Early childhood professionals also reported changed behaviors in children, including increased fear, anxiety, and an inability to concentrate (Region II Head Start Association, 2019).

Given the data, it is especially important to help children and provide them with positive coping techniques and resources in the aftermath of a disaster. These techniques can vary depending on the age of the child. The US Substance Abuse and Mental Health Services Administration (SAMHSA) offers techniques for three aged-defined categories: preschool age, early childhood, and adolescence. For our purposes, we focus on the first two categories.

Helping Preschool-Age Children

Preschool age encompasses children younger than five years. This group is unique in that they have not yet developed their own coping skills and may have a hard time verbalizing their feelings. In this age group, you may see a regression in behavior, such as a return to bedwetting or thumb sucking. You may also witness changes in sleeping habits or the child becoming more dependent on the adults in their lives. You can help these children by attempting to maintain a normal routine; providing lots of extra cuddling and verbal support; providing opportunities, such as coloring or acting, for children to express themselves; and limiting television time or exposure to the media coverage of the event (SAMHSA, n.d.).

Helping Early Childhood–Age Children

Children ages five to eleven years may also exhibit regression, have trouble concentrating at school, or show signs similar to the preschool-aged children. Be sure you are answering their questions as honestly as possible (but do not dwell on frightening details), and do not be afraid to let them know that you do not have all the answers. Lower your expectations about performance, and focus more on creating time and space for children to process the situation and information (SAMHSA, n.d.).

As you know, different children handle situations differently. Some may be eager to talk, and others may be withdrawn. Some may choose to express their feelings in play or through art. It is our job as early childhood professionals to create the opportunities for children to have the space they need to process this information and return to a sense of normalcy. Thankfully, young minds are resilient, and with proper identification of and support for mental struggles, children can recover.

With planning and preparation, you can help restore normalcy to the lives of families and children. While mental-health struggles certainly exist in the immediate aftermath of an emergency or disaster, they can also be long lasting—even lifelong. Feelings of fear, anxiety, and sadness can be reawakened by triggering events or by anniversaries. The following pages describe some of the health challenges that are encountered in a post-disaster environment. I also offer actionable tools, strategies, and resources to address mental health in the aftermath of a disaster.

Trauma and the Developing Brain

Prior to understanding the negative effects disasters and trauma can have on children, it is crucial to have a basic understanding of how trauma affects the developing brain. By the age of three, 80 percent of brain development has occurred, and by the age of five, the brain is 90 percent developed. During childhood trauma, the area of the brain that is responsible for stress response receives the most blood flow, and therefore, develops most prominently at the expense of other regions. (Garrett, 2019). When a person is under stress, the body releases adrenaline, which helps the person respond to danger. The body also releases cortisol, which also helps the body and brain cope with an adverse situation. However, if the adversity persists and the person continues to experience stress, the body continues to release cortisol and adrenaline, which can have long-term negative effects (National Scientific Council on the Developing Brain, 2014). In children, adverse childhood events (ACEs) such as trauma can decrease cognitive function, socialization, and emotional regulation. Because a child's brain is 90 percent developed by five years old, ACEs in children under five have the greatest impact on the brain in terms of its development (NC Division of Social Services, 2012). However, all youth and adolescents are vulnerable to such damage.

The more ACEs a child experiences, the greater the likelihood of developing physical and mental health problems, such as heart disease, diabetes, substance abuse, anxiety, depression, post-traumatic stress disorder (PTSD), and personality disorders, in addition to developmental and intellectual delays (DeBellis and Zisk, 2014; CDC, 2019). The levels and severity of PTSD are directly proportional to how significant the child perceived the trauma or disastrous event to be. Younger children often perceive threats to be at a higher level of danger than adolescents do. The younger the child is at the time of the disaster, the greater the probability the child will develop PTSD.

A study conducted at Duke Medical Center (De Bellis and Zisk, 2014) examined the differences in stress response of both childhood victims of trauma and those who have not experienced trauma. They concluded that because the fight-or-flight response is on overdrive in the children who experienced ACEs, the increased cortisol associated with this response reduces cognitive function and increases anxiety, aggression, and hypervigilance—all of which are symptoms associated with PTSD.

Toxic stress (a prolonged period of time in which the stress response is activated) negatively affects both physical and mental health and increases the risk for cognitive impairment throughout the lifespan of the child. Following Hurricane Katrina, for example, 60 percent of children displaced by the storm to shelters developed serious emotional disorders and/or behavioral problems (National Center for Disaster Preparedness and Children's Health Fund, 2010). Additionally, 34 percent of middle- and high-school children had their learning impacted and missed as much as a year of school (Reckdahl, 2015).

A more recent example from Puerto Rico reaches similar conclusions (Cox Marrero et al., 2018a). More than 15 percent of children experienced disturbing memories, sadness or discouragement, fear, and anxiety related to Hurricane Maria, which affected their daily well-being and functioning. In addition to the emotional pain of the hurricane, nearly 70 percent of children who were receiving treatment for a health-related condition before the storm had interruptions to their medical services due to the storm (for an average of ninety-two days). Cox Marrero and colleagues found that children under the age of five who were attending daycare or preschool missed an average of ninety-two days of daycare or preschool. This report also noted that in some cases, children experienced fear and/or lack of interest in attending daycare or preschool and had problems concentrating while at school.

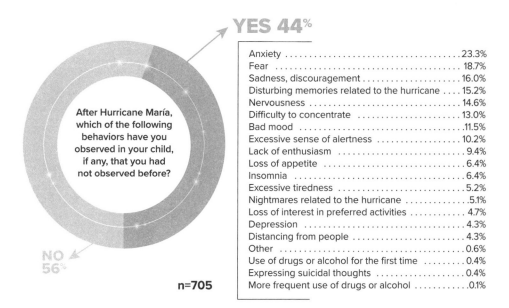

YES 44%

Anxiety	23.3%
Fear	18.7%
Sadness, discouragement	16.0%
Disturbing memories related to the hurricane	15.2%
Nervousness	14.6%
Difficulty to concentrate	13.0%
Bad mood	11.5%
Excessive sense of alertness	10.2%
Lack of enthusiasm	9.4%
Loss of appetite	6.4%
Insomnia	6.4%
Excessive tiredness	5.2%
Nightmares related to the hurricane	5.1%
Loss of interest in preferred activities	4.7%
Depression	4.3%
Distancing from people	4.3%
Other	0.6%
Use of drugs or alcohol for the first time	0.4%
Expressing suicidal thoughts	0.4%
More frequent use of drugs or alcohol	0.1%

After Hurricane María, which of the following behaviors have you observed in your child, if any, that you had not observed before?

NO 56%

n=705

Source: Cox Marrero et al., 2018b

Helping Them Heal

Early intervention is crucial to protecting the physical, mental, and emotional well-being of children who have experienced traumatic events. Supportive, responsive relationships with caring adults can reduce and potentially reverse the detrimental effects associated with stress. As child-care providers and caregivers, it is necessary to monitor for emotional dysregulation and to intervene as early as possible.

Often, caregivers do not recognize the signs of distress and when a child needs assistance with coping. Children respond differently than adults do in times of chaos, and each child may react differently from other children. On page 26, you will find a table depicting different responses to stress in relation to a child's developmental age. Of note, if the stress response occurs for greater than two to four weeks, the child may need further assistance in coping. At the end of this chapter, I offer a list of mental-health resources that offer assistance.

To help children cope after a disaster, provide them with a loving environment to establish security. Make sure the children feel safe, cared for, and loved. Offer a place where they can safely voice what may be intense emotions—and listen. Allow the children to ask questions. As developmentally appropriate, engage children in acts of service and help them take action. Even young children can donate old toys or clothes, write (or dictate) a letter to someone affected by the disaster, or help collect food and supplies to give to those who need them. Finally, but of equal importance, model positive behavior for children to emulate.

STRESS RESPONSES BY AGE

Age (Years)	Stress Responses
0–2	◦ Model caregivers' emotions ◦ Cry spontaneously ◦ Withdraw from people, avoid playtime ◦ Revert to earlier stages, such as thumb-sucking or bed-wetting if already potty-trained
3–5	◦ Show increased fear of darkness, strangers, animals, monsters, and so on ◦ Cling to caregiver ◦ Reenact trauma ◦ Revert to earlier stages, such as thumb-sucking or bed-wetting
6–10	◦ Isolate ◦ Show fear of leaving the caregiver, such as fear of school or of going to a friend's house ◦ Show aggression or irritability ◦ Have decreased concentration and school performance

Source: Adapted from Substance Abuse and Mental Health Services Administration (SAMHSA), 2018.

On May 22, 2011, an EF5 tornado struck Joplin, Missouri. Note: The Enhanced Fujita (EF) scale ranks tornadoes from EF0 (winds of 65–85 miles per hour, light damage) to EF5 (winds greater than 200 miles per hour, incredible damage). The tornado caused catastrophic damage, including destroying the home of a three-year-old girl. Weeks later, she created a new game she called "Playing Tornado." Through reenactment, she coped with the stress of losing her home and all her toys (Morris, 2011). Explaining her game, she said, "We spin in circles, and we get in a house, and we lie down, and it's blasting off, and we have to lie on the ground." According to Charles Graves, a Joplin, Missouri, psychiatrist, children will work through their mental struggles via reenactment (Morris, 2011). This allows expression of emotions in a way familiar to the child: play.

COMFORT KITS

After the Joplin tornado, the staff at Child Care Aware of Missouri created Comfort Kits. These kits included items such as lotion, bubbles, playdough, and art supplies. Each item served a distinct purpose:

- Lotion: capable of soothing children via a gentle hand and foot massage

- Bubbles: aid in deep, controlled breathing through creating many small bubbles

- Playdough: allows the child to squish it as hard as they can with their hands and feet and mold it into a shape that makes the child happy and offers a caring adult the opportunity to discuss the creation with the child

- Crayons and sketch pads: offer a creative outlet; a caring adult can suggest topics such as, "What makes you sad?" or "What calms you down?" and then discuss the drawings with the child

An important component of caring properly for children during and after a disaster is modeling positive behavior and emotions. Children need for their trusted adults to remain calm. As award-winning author and children's rights advocate L. R. Knost explains, "When little people are overwhelmed with big emotions, it is our job to share our calm, not to join their chaos." Early childhood professionals must act in the best interest of the children in their care. Although you may feel an overwhelming sense of desperation from the unrelenting chaos, you must do your best to shield the children from experiencing these emotions alongside you.

After a disaster, children often seek approval from their caregivers in terms of how they ought to think, feel, and react. Rather than expressing anxiety, fear, and anger in front of children, remove yourself when necessary to calm your emotions. Then, express yourself in a positive, collected manner with the children. Foster a safe space where the children can freely talk about their feelings rather than holding back. Model resilience in the face of challenges with the hope that the children will learn from your example. Remember, while children should not see *your* full range of emotions after a disaster, it's important to emphasize that it is healthy for *them* to express exactly how they are feeling whenever a particular emotion arises.

Unfortunately, you will encounter numerous triggers that will elicit emotions in children impacted by a disaster. Children's emotions may be triggered by the anniversary of the event; specific smells, locations, and sounds; or media coverage of the disaster. Therefore, encourage an open environment in which a child has a safe place to decompress after such reminders. The media generally discusses sensational aspects related to an event. Often included in this coverage are emotion-stirring images and close-up videos. Young children are unable to comprehend that the images and videos displayed are from the event that has already occurred instead of an additional disaster that is striking again.

For instance, if footage of the aftermath of a tornado is aired in the media, a child may have difficulty understanding that what is shown is the same tornado that has already left its devastating impact, not another one that is about to destroy the town again. Consequently, a child may feel as though she is in danger again. Commonly reported effects from disaster media coverage include anger, fear, worry, sadness, decreased concentration, inability to fall or to stay asleep, and increased attachment to caregivers. Therefore, following a disaster, child-care professionals should limit and monitor children's exposure to media coverage.

As always, allow the children to ask questions. Because children are very inquisitive, they will try to comprehend why something occurred, especially when they lack sufficient information or experience to understand. Answer these questions as honestly as you can, without creating unnecessary fear or a sense of danger. Do your best to avoid blaming any one person or group for what may have happened; nothing good comes from scapegoating or generalizing. Do not be afraid to let children know that you do not have all the answers. It is better to be honest and trustworthy than to promote a lie or mistruth. Help children identify the good things that are happening around them. This can include the helpers who have come in to assist after the disaster. Encourage open conversations and provide reassurance that you are doing all you can to protect the children and keep them safe. The National Association for the Education of Young Children (NAEYC) offers more tips at https://www.naeyc.org/system/files/11tips_11.3.pdf

Avoiding Burnout

Each disaster recovery is unique, even for those who respond to disasters. I spent nearly eight years as a firefighter-paramedic in the Chicagoland area. During that time, I saw a lot of trauma and grief. Of course, this was expected, as individuals typically call 911 during one of the worst moments of their lives. The focus at the fire department was different than what we are talking about in this book. At the fire department, we would respond to an emergency call, such as a house fire. We would get to the scene and do what we could to limit death, harm, and destruction. Usually within an hour or two, the fire was out and the scene was under control. We would then pack up the hoses and equipment and return to the fire station to await the next call. This type of emergency response is totally different than what is experienced and encountered in disaster recovery.

Disaster recovery should be thought of as a marathon, not a sprint. The days are long, often with little visible progress from day to day. This environment leads to burnout and prolonged stress. It is also important to note that even if your home or business did not get completely destroyed, there is a high probability that the building will be uninhabitable, especially for children, for a period of time. Having workers on your property is distracting, and even something as simple as fixing cracks in drywall and repainting can require you to vacate the property.

My family experienced this firsthand, and we were forced to live elsewhere for several months. The daily hammering, saws running, drywall dust flying around, fumes from paint and from refinishing the floors, and other disturbances were certainly not a place for a three-week-old baby. The situation would have definitely made naptime difficult, but more importantly, it would have also negatively affected her health and well-being.

Meeting Basic Needs

If you are not familiar with the work of Abraham Maslow, he was a psychologist who developed a theory about what motivates humans. His 1943 article "A Theory of Human Motivation" describes a hierarchy of human needs. In a nutshell, he says that the most basic needs—food, shelter, water, rest, safety—must be satisfied before a person can focus on other needs such as developing relationships, self-esteem, learning, and creativity. I believe it is worth noting that many people in post-disaster situations are dealing with meeting their most basic needs: stable housing, access to healthy foods, and rest. Each of these needs can be difficult, and sometimes impossible, to fulfill after a disaster.

The little (and not-so-little) inconveniences of post-disaster life add up over time and can create prolonged stress—referred to as *chronic stress*. Unlike short-term stress, such as that of responding to and putting out a house fire, chronic stress does not go away in a few hours. It stays with you and affects you each day. This type of environment can lead to burnout or even compassion fatigue.

To navigate the challenging period after a disaster, keep some tips in mind. First, remember that the situation you are living through is likely a completely new challenge, maybe even one you never imagined having to face. It is new to you, your families, and your staff. Each of you is doing the best you can to rebuild and recover. It sometimes helps each day to just say the words out loud: "I am doing the best I can." If you are a perfectionist or a person who loves being in control, this will be an especially challenging time. Although easier said than done, now is the time to lower your expectations for yourself and everyone around you. Each individual is going to be coming to this challenge in their own unique way; allow everyone enough time and space to do so. Understand that no one is going to be functioning at their normal levels or to the fullest of their abilities.

If friends and family offer help (which they likely will), be specific and honest about your challenges and what you need. Unless a person has personally experienced a disaster and its aftermath, it is very difficult to put oneself in the shoes of someone who is dealing with such a crisis. Some family members or friends may downplay what you are experiencing and feeling; others may become distant because they are giving you space. I have found that the best way to handle this is to be specific and honest about what you are going through, your challenges, and how they can help. Sometimes there may be nothing they can do except listen and provide support from afar.

Try not to compare your recovery and rebuilding process to others'. Personally, I found it hard to not compare my home and my progress to those of the people around me. I am also a bit ashamed to admit that sometimes I would feel jealous that others nearby were seemingly light years ahead of where we were in terms of disaster restoration and getting their property back to normal. This is a typical reaction. At the outset, you have to remind yourself and come to terms with the fact that different homes and types of properties are going to progress at different paces. This does not mean anyone is "winning," only that certain supplies and skilled workers are easier to get than others.

This is especially true in areas that already lack skilled labor and supplies prior to a disaster. For instance, rebuilding and recovery in Puerto Rico and the USVI faced massive delays in supplies and equipment. Nearly everything must arrive via boat to these islands, and that process certainly takes time. However, there is another factor to be taken into account and a lesson to be learned: Our supply chains are not responsive enough to handle a sudden influx of demand. Remember the great toilet-paper shortage of 2020, when COVID-19 lockdown orders sent shoppers racing to stores to purchase toilet paper? It took months for the supply chain to recover. In short, try to keep a positive outlook during this difficult time—even if your neighbor is seemingly making more progress than you. At the end of the day, all progress is good progress in restoring the overall community.

Compassion Fatigue

A common occurrence in disaster-relief workers is *vicarious traumatization*, or secondary traumatization (Adams, Boscarino, and Figley, 2006). Simply put, this term refers to the "emotional residue" or strain of exposure to working with those suffering from the consequences of disasters or traumatic events. For example, if you live in an area that experiences a disaster, but your home or business was not significantly affected, you may end up having compassion fatigue. Likewise, if you are serving children who have undergone a disaster, but you have not personally endured such an event, the same phenomenon may come into play as well.

Compassion fatigue does not always have to be specifically disaster related. It can and does exist for individuals who serve victims of abuse, or in any situation that requires comforting and understanding. Studies show that from 6 percent to 26 percent of therapists who work with traumatized populations, and up to 50 percent of child-welfare workers, may be at risk from this type of situation (Sprang and Ross, 2011). Compassion fatigue has been described as the cost of caring. Essentially, you care so much that you begin to personally take on the challenges and trauma of those you are trying to help.

The following are a few warning signs of compassion fatigue:

- Mental or emotional exhaustion
- Reduced sense of personal accomplishment or meaning in work
- Trouble sleeping
- Isolation/decreased interactions with others
- Anger toward routine or casual events
- Loss of self-worth

Ideally, we recognize the toll that these events are taking on us well in advance. However, knowing the signs is often easier than doing something about them.

Self-Care After a Disaster

Several techniques that you can add to your daily or weekly routine may help you avoid compassion fatigue or burnout. These are commonly called self-help or self-care techniques and allow you to focus inward, making sure you are in touch with your feelings and mental and emotional well-being.

Many mental-health professionals encourage the use of a self-care plan. This allows you to develop, on paper, a plan you can follow to ensure you are taking steps to care for your emotional and mental well-being. Having the plan written down on paper also provides a mechanism for you to hold yourself accountable for completing the elements of your plan.

There is no right or wrong self-care plan. Essentially, you are trying to sketch out the best way for *you* to manage stress and achieve balance in *your* life. Your plan should address the welfare of your mind, body, and spirit, and it should serve as a reminder of the things that make you feel good.

- Think about what your ideal day would look like.

  › What time would you wake up?

  › What would you have for breakfast?

  › What types of activities make you feel good? going for a walk? doing yoga? listening to a podcast? watching a television show? reading a book? prayer or meditation? exercise? chatting with a close friend?

  › What time would you ideally go to sleep?

- Once you have identified the ideal day, you can begin to use it as a guide. If you are feeling off, refer to your self-care plan. Pick out a few things you can do to help make yourself feel better.

The goal is not necessarily to do everything on your list each day but to have more awareness about when you are and are not doing these things. No matter how stressful or busy your days become, it is important for your mental and emotional well-being that you make yourself a priority.

MENTAL HEALTH RESOURCES

Childhelp National Child-Abuse Hotline: 1-800-4 A CHILD (1-800-422-4453)
https://www.childwelfare.gov/aboutus/find-help/

"Helping Students Cope with Media Coverage of Disasters," video, Terrorism and Disaster Center, University of Missouri:
https://www.youtube.com/watch?v=BqYZMYqsLqQ

MentalHealth.gov: https://www.mentalhealth.gov/

Institute for Childhood Preparedness:
https://www.childhoodpreparedness.org/recovery

SAMHSA Disaster Distress Helpline (English and Spanish): 1-800-985-5990
https://www.samhsa.gov/find-help/disaster-distress-helpline

SAMHSA mental health resources: 1-800-662-HELP (1-800-662-4357)
https://www.samhsa.gov/

Helping Hands in the Community

We are very lucky to have so many wonderful people and organizations that are willing to donate their time and resources to help post-disaster. It is indeed impressive how busloads of volunteers unselfishly descend on an area to help. Although these volunteers are certainly well intentioned, without proper coordination, this influx of people into a damaged area can also create additional stress on the community.

As with any practice, there are various levels of skill and organization among groups. Also, it is likely that individuals who are not affiliated with a group will show up because they want to assist in some way. Unorganized groups and individuals who self-deploy to an area can create challenges. The best volunteers are individuals who have prepared and been trained to respond and who do not require any external resources for support. Essentially, this means bringing your own food, water, sleeping accommodations, tools, and equipment. The goal is to be self-sustaining—that way you are not taking away any resources that could be used to support the individuals directly impacted by the disaster.

Different challenges will arise, depending on the size and location of the disaster. For example, recovery from a small, localized tornado could be supported from a nearby community. Volunteers could drive in from surrounding communities, work during the day, and then return to their respective homes or communities each night. On the other hand, for widespread damage or in areas of limited access, such as the Florida Keys or Puerto Rico, the challenge is more significant. In these cases, volunteers will need to consider sleeping arrangements—often in tents or recreational vehicles (RVs)—as well as carefully preplan logistical needs, such as food, water, and gasoline.

Volunteer Coordination

Coordination of volunteers is a science in and of itself. Fortunately, groups exist that specialize in volunteer management during disaster response and recovery. One of the organizations you should be familiar with is called Voluntary Organizations Active in Disaster (VOAD). Many organizations fall under the VOAD umbrella, including governmental, private-sector, nonprofit, and religious entities. The services provided by these groups vary, but the role of VOAD is to serve as a coordinating body to help ensure efforts are as efficient and effective as possible.

National VOAD (https://www.nvoad.org/about-us) was founded in response to the challenges seen during the aftermath of Hurricane Camille, a Category 5 storm that struck the Gulf Coast in 1969. The need was evident for this type of coordinating body. While there was no shortage of volunteers offering assistance, the help was often not getting to the right places, as independent organizations were uncoordinated and in many cases duplicated each other's efforts.

There are currently fifty-six VOADs that serve the states and territories of the United States. In some large metropolitan areas, local VOADs also support the efforts of cities or counties. These VOADs meet regularly, even in nondisaster times, to ensure continued coordination and cooperation of all parties involved. During times of disaster, the state or regional VOAD serves in a coordination role and acts as a clearinghouse of information, allowing the relief organizations to focus their energies and expertise on activities in the impacted area.

While there are many members of VOAD, the following describe a few select participating organizations and their capabilities to help provide some context.

- Adventist Community Services (ACS) volunteers provide disaster-response services through the ACS Disaster Response Ministry to assist individuals, families, and communities affected by natural and manmade disasters and unforeseen tragedies. ACS has developed an expertise in donations management through multiagency warehouses and collection and distribution centers. During other responses, ACS has assisted as requested by feeding survivors and first responders, providing chainsaw teams, participating in debris cleanup and mucking out, providing temporary roofing, setting up spontaneous-volunteer reception centers, and offering in-home repair as part of long-term recovery.

- The American Red Cross is a well-known emergency and disaster-response organization. In addition to immediate response, they also provide assistance with recovery by offering a variety of services, which can vary by location. These services may include providing emergency financial assistance in the immediate aftermath of a disaster, distributing financial assistance for households that need extra help in the long term, and providing grants for community-based recovery services.

- Catholic Charities USA is the official domestic relief agency of the US Catholic Church. Its disaster-response team helps assist and provide disaster relief. Catholic Charities offers an array of services, from assisting with temporary housing to helping with reunification to providing counseling services. This organization often coordinates with local and/or regional faith-based organizations to strengthen the impact of its work.

- Lutheran Disaster Response is one of the few organizations that has helped to provide child care in the aftermath of a disaster. It also offers additional services, such as providing emotional and spiritual care for people who have been affected by a disaster and for leaders who respond to a disaster. They coordinate volunteers through local affiliates and churches and provide long-term recovery efforts by addressing the unmet needs months or even years after a disaster strikes.

- Save the Children is an international organization that provides assistance across the world and also responds domestically to disasters and emergencies. Depending on the situation, its volunteers may provide child-care services for families in need, such as families at a shelter or a disaster-recovery center. Save the Children often provides essential items for children, such as hygiene kits, diapers, wipes, and portable cribs.

As you can see, the VOADs bring in a tremendous amount of resources, tools, funding, and other assistance. Like many organizations, they sometimes can forget about the needs of early childhood programs. Early engagement before a disaster can help ensure that the needs of children and early childhood programs are included in disaster and recovery planning efforts. Most VOADs have websites that contain their contact information. The National VOAD also keeps records of the various state- and territory-level VOADs.

Here are some important questions you could ask a VOAD:

- What resources are available to assist your early childhood program after a disaster?
- Are they capable of offering child care, in case your program needs to close for a period of time? This could be good information to pass along to parents.
- Do they have any potential alternate sites where your early childhood program could be temporarily located after a disaster? If so, do the sites have generators?
- What types of training are available? Many VOADs and their partner organizations offer disaster training that may be beneficial to you and/or your staff.
- Do they offer supplies that may be beneficial for children to have after a disaster? For example, does the VOAD have ready access to diapers, formula, baby food, toys, and other goods?
- If interested, ask if you could speak or present at one of the upcoming VOAD meetings. It is always nice when organizations get to learn more about the work that early childhood programs and caregivers perform and the unique needs we may have after a disaster.
- Are there any local philanthropic organizations that may offer grants to increase preparedness efforts?
- What is the best way to coordinate with the VOAD during a time of disaster? Remember, you do not want to be exchanging business cards during an emergency. The more contacts you can identify ahead of time, the better.

Donations

In addition to well-meaning volunteers, something else often floods disaster-impacted areas: stuff. Donations after disasters can certainly be useful, but in many cases the donated stuff becomes a second disaster—one that is time-consuming and costly to manage. Imagine a situation in which your home or business is destroyed or cannot be occupied. You are struggling day to day to identify places where you can safely live and where you can store and secure any undamaged possessions. Then comes the influx of donated items—many of which you never asked for and probably will never need or use. One study (Holguín-Veras et al., 2014) found that between 50 and 70 percent of items that arrive during a disaster are not needed or are inappropriate for the recovery or the geographical region. The donations shown in the photograph were not requested and ended up adding to the already large pile of garbage and debris that needed to be disposed of.

Handling Unneeded Donations

In Newtown, Connecticut, after the Sandy Hook Elementary School shooting in 2012, more than 65,000 teddy bears (including over 1,000 life-sized ones), along with over half a million cards, were received (Herzog, 2018). This influx presented tremendous logistical challenges for a small community of 27,000 people—donors sent more than two teddy bears for every resident! In addition to trying to console a heartbroken community, support organizations had to use their resources to manage the incredible volume of unsolicited donations. The influx quickly overwhelmed the local post office. Eventually, 80,000 square feet of warehouse space was secured just to house all these donations.

In 2017, wildfires in California destroyed approximately 10,000 homes. Many residents were able to evacuate from the area, but some stayed behind and took refuge at a local community shelter. One shelter in Petaluma housed 100 displaced individuals. In less than twenty-four hours, the shelter received numerous unsolicited donations, including 5,000 toothbrushes and 3,000 sticks of deodorant. Obviously, this was much more than the displaced individuals could use, and these unsolicited donations had to be relocated and stored (Rudolph, n.d.).

When a horrific earthquake struck Haiti in 2010, the donations came pouring in. This time, things were a little different: because Haiti is on an island, all donations had to be sent via airplane. The plethora of "stuff" not only tied up cargo space for more appropriate and valuable supplies, but it also led to a logistical issue at the airport where space was at a premium. There are numerous stories of inappropriate items that arrived in Haiti, including ten shipping containers of refrigerators—which were of no use as there was no power and many individuals were living in tents. According to a report from the United Nations Office for the Coordination of Humanitarian Affairs, other mismatched donations included winter clothes (for a tropical island!), potato chips, energy drinks, and even tuxedos (Boulet-Desbareau, 2013).

I also saw winter clothes arriving in Puerto Rico during my time working on the island following Hurricanes Maria and Irma. Estimates are that clothing makes up 40 percent to 50 percent of all disaster donations (Gammon, 2012). Most of the time the clothing is unusable and ends up in a landfill.

While many donations are sent by well-meaning individuals who are truly trying to help after a disaster, sometimes the donations are not as sincere. Worse, some businesses take advantage of a disaster as an opportunity to offload unneeded or even dangerous inventory. For example, one situation involved an unsolicited load of cribs sent to a disaster recovery center. It was soon discovered that these cribs had been made overseas and contained high levels of toxic chemicals in the paint—definitely not something you want to expose a young child to. Not every corporation engages in this type of behavior, obviously. But for those that do, they have an opportunity to receive a tax break, offload inventory, and potentially get some good press for "assisting" a community in need. Not everyone has pure motives.

There is no magic solution to prevent unwanted donations from being delivered to your facility. Try as you may, it is likely that some donations are simply going to "show up." There are a few things you can do to help minimize the amount of unwanted donations. For example, work with a trusted community organization that is handling disaster donations. Contacting them early and letting them know what you need—and, importantly, what you do not need—can help ensure unwanted items do not reach your doorstep. Be open and honest about your needs. Use social media and your emailing lists to inform others of your status and ways they might help. If you need something, do not be afraid to ask for it. When describing the agreement that Banana Cabana in the Florida Keys made with the local elementary school to temporarily provide classrooms for children in child care, Roxanne Rosado said it best: "You won't know an answer unless you ask." Roxanne's wisdom is worth repeating. After a disaster is not a time to be shy when it comes to expressing what is needed to help you, your staff, and—most important—the children you care for.

Cash Is King

The big takeaway here is that, after a disaster, cash really is king. Providing cash donations to reputable organizations that are actively working in the disaster area is, by far, the biggest help. For a concrete illustration, the United States Agency for International Development (USAID) and its Center for International Disaster Information (CIDI) uses its own "Greatest Good Donations Calculator" that takes into account the cost of actually transporting donations into a disaster area (CIDI USAID, n.d.). For example, sending bottled water overseas can be up to 1,000 times more expensive than producing drinkable water locally, according to the calculator. Further, sending a twenty-dollar teddy bear from Los Angeles, California, to Delhi, India, would actually end up costing $165.85. A cash donation would be much more helpful.

For a real-world look at how donations can help restore and reopen a child care program, visit https://www.childhoodpreparedness.org/recovery and watch the Florida Keys video featuring the Banana Cabana early childhood program.

Examples like the ones above really highlight how much waste there can be in disaster donations. Conversely, cash donations are easy to perform and are safe and secure. They offer the maximum flexibility and allow organizations that are actively on the ground to acquire supplies and items that can truly benefit the impacted individuals. As a bonus, spending the cash in the affected community, as often happens, helps support local businesses that may be struggling after a disaster.

6

Health and Safety Considerations

Before a disaster happens, health and safety are aspects of preparation that are critical to consider for a multitude of reasons. Supplies may be scarce right after a disaster occurs due to other individuals obtaining the requisite supplies first. Power outages in the surrounding area, inaccessibility of roads, a dangerous climate, and chaos due to public fear may prevent you from getting the supplies you need. However, with adequate preparation, you can have the supplies you will require, such as an emergency food and water supply, first-aid supplies, and items for maintaining personal hygiene.

In book 2 of the Preparing for the Unexpected series, *Preschool Preparedness for an Emergency*, I offer details on creating, testing, and revising your emergency plan.

Food and Water Supplies

To be fully prepared for a disaster, it is important to have an adequate water supply, as water supplies may be compromised due to damaged water mains, the inability to access well water, and a plethora of other reasons. To prepare an emergency supply of water, we recommend you store at least one gallon of drinking water per day per person (and per pet). If you reside in a hot and humid climate, you may consider storing additional water. It is recommended that you prepare for three days of interrupted supply, so you should have on hand a total of at least three gallons of water per person and per pet. Unopened, commercially bottled water is the safest and most reliable emergency supply.

In the event that bottled water is not available, the CDC recommends using one of the methods outlined here. The CDC (2021c) states that the best method is boiling water for 1 minute (or 3 minutes if located at elevations above 6,500 feet) to kill any potential contamination by bacteria, viruses, and parasites. Water also can be disinfected by using bleach, so you will want to secure unscented liquid household chlorine bleach to use for this purpose. To properly disinfect the water, add eight drops (or a little less than ⅛ of a teaspoon) of 5–6 percent unscented household bleach to one gallon of water, mix well, and then wait at least 30 minutes prior to using (CDC, 2021c). Be sure to store the bleach where the temperature is around 70 degrees F (21 degrees C) in a place inaccessible to children.

Food can also be hard to come by. Grocery stores are often damaged or without power, leading to a scarcity of food available for purchase. In other cases, the grocery store may be destroyed or unable to open because staff cannot reach the location.

Before a disaster happens, plan for a three-day supply of food. Foods well equipped for this supply include those with a long shelf life that require no cooking water or refrigeration, such as ready-to-eat canned meats, fruits, and vegetables; protein bars; vacuum-sealed fruit snacks; and dry cereal. Additionally, be sure to include foods that meet any special dietary needs. To decrease the need for additional drinking water, store foods that are low in salt and spice content. Be sure to store items in secured boxes and bins that are waterproof and airtight to protect from water, rodents, and insects. Also have on hand eating utensils, a manual can opener, dish soap, hand soap, and a 60-percent-alcohol hand sanitizer.

Post-disaster, discard perishable food items that have not been properly refrigerated or frozen, as well as any food that has contacted floodwater or storm water or has an unusual odor, color, or texture. An unopened refrigerator will keep food safe for up to four hours without power. A full freezer left unopened will maintain safe food for forty-eight hours, and an unopened half-full freezer will keep food for twenty-four hours. It is essential to keep the refrigerator and freezer doors closed as often as possible. Opening the doors releases the cold air and raises the internal temperature, increasing the speed at which food will be rendered inedible.

For commercially prepared food in cans and pouches, remove labels after noting the expiration dates. Secondly, brush and wipe away dirt and silt, and then wash the cans and pouches thoroughly with hot, soapy water. We recommend you also sanitize the packaging by placing each item in five cups of water with one cup of unscented household bleach; another sanitizing method is to place the item in a pot of boiling water for at least two minutes. After thorough cleaning and sanitizing, relabel the cans and pouches with the specific expiration dates.

Personal Hygiene

In addition to securing nonperishable food and clean drinking water, it is also necessary to maintain personal hygiene during an emergency. Personal hygiene and handwashing are crucial to preventing the spread of illness and disease, especially during a natural disaster. During a boil-water advisory or a do-not-drink-water advisory, you may still be able to safely wash your hands with soap and tap water (CDC, 2021b). If local authorities recommend extreme caution, wash with soap and water that has been boiled and cooled or disinfected with one cup of bleach for every five gallons of water. If washing with soap and water is not possible, be sure to use your alcohol-based hand sanitizer that you stored with your emergency food supply. If you're ever unsure about the safety and quality of your water after a disaster, contact your local health department or your local authorities for detailed information.

General Supplies

Further, it would be advantageous for early childhood providers to keep general supplies in storage for use if necessary. While this list is not meant to be exhaustive, examples of additional items to include are a flashlight, extra batteries, a portable battery charger for cell phones, a whistle to signal for help, glow sticks for light (children love these), a wrench or pliers to turn off utilities, extra changes of clothes for the children in your care, extra toys for the children, local maps (especially a map to your evacuation locations), moist towelettes, garbage bags, duct tape, contact information for each of the children and the staff members, photos of the children (in case anyone gets lost or separated), and a sleeping bag or warm blanket for each person. Additionally, it is important to consider the location of your early childhood care program, as needs may vary depending upon your local climate.

First Aid

Unfortunately, injuries are common during and after disasters. Nails, jagged edges, and construction debris can cause cuts, abrasions, and more serious injuries. Exposure to toxic substances, such as leaking gas from broken natural gas lines, can cause serious illness. The consequences of these exposures suggest additional reasons why it is essential to maintain proper hygiene, if possible. Further, it is extremely important to ensure a first-aid kit is available in case of an emergency situation. Luckily, the majority of early childhood programs should have these on hand, as they are often a licensure requirement. Each licensing jurisdiction will require different components to be included in the first-aid kit. Where applicable, follow your licensing requirements. Caring for Our Children also has a list of recommended items, including adhesive bandages, tape, antiseptic solution (hydrogen peroxide), disposable latex-free gloves, fever-reducing medications (such as acetaminophen and ibuprofen), tweezers, two liters of sterile water for cleaning wounds or eyes, and scissors (National Resource Center for Health and Safety in Child Care and Early Education, 2020).

In 2016, an EF3 tornado, with winds reaching up to 152 miles per hour, struck Kokomo, Indiana. Twenty homes were destroyed, and eighteen suffered major damage. Family child-care provider Ms. Jill was at work in her family home. Ms. Jill was kind enough to provide an in-person interview about her terrifying experience and how she kept the children in her care calm and safe. She also provided actionable tips for early childhood professionals on supplies and equipment to keep close at hand. In discussing why she takes preparedness so seriously, she said, "These kids are my family. I have other people's babies; this is their heart on my floor." Watch Ms. Jill's entire interview on https://www.childhoodpreparedness.org/recovery

While all states require that all early childhood professionals become certified in CPR, the Red Cross has steps written out on their website (https://www.redcross.org/take-a-class/cpr/performing-cpr/cpr-steps) just in case you need a quick reminder. If unsure of how to care for a wound, you can also consult the national CPR Foundation's website here: https://www.nationalcprfoundation.com/courses/standard-first-aid-3/introduction/.

Disclaimer: these websites are only meant to assist in an emergency situation when there is not a medical doctor or competent healthcare professional available. Do not use these websites in place of a medical doctor or in place of any training required by your licensing authority.

Tetanus

One potentially fatal infection that can result from wounds and cuts that are improperly cared for is tetanus. In fact, one out of five people diagnosed with tetanus will die from it. Tetanus is caused by *Clostridium tetani*, a bacterium that infects wounds that are contaminated with soil, feces, saliva, and rust. Rusty screws, nails, and debris are common sources of tetanus after natural disasters (Afshar, Raju, Ansell, and Bleck, 2011).

Symptoms of tetanus include muscle spasms, muscle pain, and difficulty swallowing and breathing, which may lead to death. While tetanus is an expected complication after disasters in developing nations, the condition is less common, although still a threat, in the United States. Nearly universal vaccinations in the United States have lessened the frequency of infections here; tetanus affects a wider range of individuals in developing countries due to lack of vaccines. Be sure to follow your state's guidelines for tetanus vaccinations in the children enrolled in your program. Children should receive a three-dose series at ages two, four, and six months, followed by a booster between fifteen and eighteen months of age, and again from four to six years old. After the childhood series, it is recommended that people receive a booster vaccination every ten years (CDC, 2020).

Regardless of vaccination status, it is vital to properly clean all cuts and wounds. If possible, wash the wounds with soap and water and apply a topical antibiotic ointment. Once sanitized, wrap the wound to prevent bacteria from contaminating it. However, if you are unable to disinfect the wound, do not wrap it. If you cover an unclean wound, you are trapping bacteria and increasing the likelihood of developing a serious infection or diseases.

Carbon Monoxide

Another potential health crisis following disasters is carbon monoxide poisoning. Carbon monoxide is an odorless, colorless gas and may be fatal if inhaled. Common sources of carbon monoxide include gas furnaces, oil-burning furnaces, portable generators, and charcoal grills. While these are common household items, you should use them with extreme caution.

Never use a generator, charcoal grill, or other gasoline, propane, or charcoal-burning device inside a home or garage, even if the doors and windows remain open. All these items should be kept a minimum of twenty feet away from the home, doors, windows, and garages. Additionally, when using these items, be sure to have a battery-powered carbon monoxide detector in the building (CDC, 2017).

Common symptoms of carbon monoxide poisoning include a cherry-red face and flu-like symptoms, such as headache, nausea and vomiting, diarrhea, weakness, chest pain, and confusion. Seek medical care immediately if you suspect carbon monoxide poisoning, as it is rapidly fatal. Also, be sure to evacuate the area entirely.

The CDC and Research Triangle Institute conducted a review of disaster-related carbon monoxide poisoning (Iqbal et al, 2008). The studies reviewed described a total of 362 incidents and 1,888 cases of disaster-related carbon monoxide poisoning, as well as a reported seventy-five fatalities. The reviewers found that, on average, for every incident reported, two people were affected. Generators were the primary source of carbon monoxide exposure, accounting for 83 percent of the fatalities and 54 percent of nonfatal cases. Of those generator-caused fatalities, 67 percent were due to the improper usage of generators inside a building.

Another example highlighting the detrimental impact of carbon monoxide poisoning after disasters pertains to Hurricane Ida. Three days after Ida swept through New Orleans, seven children and five adults were stricken with carbon monoxide poisoning in a single home where a generator was not properly used. Similarly, nine individuals were hospitalized from a different home because of using a generator in a garage attached to their home. Many were poisoned with carbon monoxide after Ida, and at least ten individuals died (WWL Staff, 2021). If you use a generator, charcoal grill, or other gasoline, propane, or charcoal-burning device, be sure to use it outdoors, well away from your building.

Radon

Like carbon monoxide, radon is an odorless and colorless gas that damages health. Radon is a naturally occurring radioactive gas released from the natural decay of uranium found in rock and soil. Radon often becomes a health crisis during earthquakes. While earthquakes do not directly create radon, the disruption of rock and soil during an earthquake causes cracks and damages to foundations of buildings, releasing the existing gas (3R's Construction, n.d.).

Low levels of radon can generally be detected in lower stories and basements of homes; it is the second leading cause of lung cancer in the United States, responsible for more than 20,000 lung cancer–related deaths every year. Both the US Environmental Protection Agency (EPA, n.d.) and the US Surgeon General (US Department of Health and Human Services, 2005) have recommended all buildings, including homes and early childhood facilities, be tested for radon.

However, after earthquakes, even if structural damage is not visibly apparent, it's important to test and confirm the level of radon. Radon testing kits are available at numerous locations, including hardware stores and online from the National Radon Program Services. It is vital to understand that the longer the exposure to radon, the higher the probability of developing lung cancer as an adult. If children are exposed to radon many hours a day throughout their childhood, they are at significant risk of lung cancer.

Flooding

Another potential post-disaster health crisis follows flooding. In 2017, after Hurricane Harvey struck Texas and Louisiana, six feet or more of floodwater damaged not only structures but also playgrounds. Floodwaters can contain raw sewage, animal carcasses, and debris. They can also harbor a wide variety of harmful pollutants such as chemicals, bacteria, parasites, and even viruses. These can cause bodily harm and/or infection, such as gastrointestinal illnesses, skin infections, and Legionnaire's disease, if they enter the body through the mouth, eyes, or a cut in the skin.

When floodwaters recede, it is important to inspect all play areas thoroughly (Sheperd, 2017). Remove all debris. Hose down all equipment with clean water to ensure the chemicals and other pollutants from floodwater have been washed away. Conduct a thorough inspection and remove or secure any loose nails and equipment. The goal is to allow children to safely play on playgrounds after natural disasters, and the first step in restoring a piece of normalcy is to ensure a safe place to play.

7 Communication

Communication after a disaster is essential. Unfortunately, communication may prove difficult, especially if critical telecommunications infrastructure has been damaged. As part of your overall preparedness-planning efforts, develop a crisis-communications plan that covers the need to send information out during and after emergencies and disasters.

During storms and other natural disasters, cellular towers can be damaged or destroyed. For example, during Hurricane Katrina, nearly two thousand cell phone tower sites failed, and during Hurricane Maria, 95 percent failed (Committee on Homeland Security, 2005; Chavez, 2017; Scott, 2018). These numbers stress the need for a multimodal communication strategy—one that includes communication methods such as landline telephones, telephone calling trees (in which one person is responsible for passing the message to others, who then pass it on to others), and cellular phones. It is also wise to include other communication methods, such as email, social media, and texting. As previously noted, it is a good idea to keep a battery-powered phone charger and/or a vehicle cell-phone charger in your emergency kit. There are also solar-powered phone chargers readily available for sale.

Communication is the single biggest point of failure in an emergency or disaster. It is an essential service and one which requires training and testing. Communication encompasses a wide variety of actions: internal communication, stakeholder communication, parental communication, media communication, and staff communication, just to name a few.

In advance of a disaster, early childhood programs should compile contact information for each of these audiences into a database that is accessible during an emergency. This database should be updated regularly and shared with a few trusted individuals within your organization. The database should include contact information for enrolled families, suppliers, building management (if in a rented space), government officials (such as licensing, the fire marshal, the health department), your staff and employees, and the media.

In all these types of communications, strive for unity of messaging. *Unity of messaging* means putting out similar, nonconflicting information for both internal and external use. In today's society, information moves rapidly. It is incumbent on our organizations to ensure that the information presented is timely and accurate. This leads to trust and credibility.

Government organizations study how to respond to disaster and crisis situations and have developed the term *crisis emergency risk communications* (CERC) to describe communications during a disaster. CERC identifies six important principles for communicating during times of high stress:

- **Be first:** Quickly providing information during a disaster is important. People usually remember what they hear first, and you want your clients, customers, families, and staff to hear information about your program from you, not from rumors or speculation.

- **Be right:** As we have discussed in other areas of this book, trust is a very important factor in the post-disaster environment. You want to ensure your messages are honest and accurate; otherwise, you risk damaging your reputation. It is an emergency, so there is a good chance you may not have all the information, and that is okay. But you should acknowledge this in your messaging.

- **Be credible:** Similar to being right, you want to be the credible, trusted source of information, especially when it relates to your business or early childhood program.

- **Express empathy:** During disasters, some individuals will get injured and perhaps badly hurt. Others may lose their homes or livelihood. You want your compassion to shine through during these times. You want to address what people, such as the families that you serve, are feeling and the particular challenges that they may face in the future. This is a chance to bring everyone together as one family.

- **Promote action:** This one can be difficult, but in a disaster, people are looking for something they can do. Taking action helps individuals feel like they are contributing and making the situation better. It also occupies the mind and can reduce stress or anxiety. Sometimes, the best action is no action, and simply saying, "Hug your children," or "Keep those impacted in your thoughts," may be all the action you can offer.

- **Show respect:** Disasters cause vulnerabilities, and you must ensure that your communications are respectful at all times. Do not get into the "blame game," especially in the immediate aftermath of a disaster.
  (CDC, 2014)

As part of your crisis plan, establish a contact who can help with your communication efforts. Ideally this person would live out of your area. That way if an emergency does happen, it is unlikely to impact both you and your emergency communication person. For example, if you live in Chicago, you could designate a family member who lives in Indianapolis as your emergency contact person. Given the distance, it is unlikely that a disaster would affect both geographic areas. This means the emergency contact would likely still have power, internet, and cell-phone service and could assist by sending emails, posting social-media messages, and the like on your behalf. Obviously, such coordination requires planning ahead of time and ensuring the emergency communication contact person has the proper credentials to send and/or post messages for you and your organization.

A good way to help plan for an emergency situation is to walk through the various challenges you would face during and after a disaster that may impact your program. For example, if you live in an area where ice storms, earthquakes, hurricanes, or tornadoes happen, work with your staff and emergency out-of-area contact to develop a strategy for how you would handle communications if this type of emergency were to occur.

Likewise, you can anticipate that certain audiences are going to seek certain information. For example, parents will want to know the answers to questions such as the following:

- Are my children okay?
- How is this going to impact me and my family?
- Can this be fixed? When can this be fixed?
- What will we do in the immediate aftermath for our child-care needs?

On the other hand, the media is going to want to know answers to questions such as the following:

- What happened here?
- Are there any victims? Are they being helped?
- What can the public do to help?
- Who is in charge here?
- What is the plan going forward?

Remember, the media is generally after the who, what, where, why, when, and how for each story that they cover.

HANDLING THE MEDIA

Part of your communication plan should address who is allowed to speak to the media. Disasters are media events, and during a disaster, the media will interview anyone and everyone that they can. There should be a clear understanding of who is allowed to speak to the staff and who is not. Also, the media works on deadlines. They want to get the information as soon as possible. Sometimes the complexity of a disaster makes this difficult. If you do not know the information or are still working to assess the situation, there are some simple phrases you can use with the media without saying, "No comment."

First, always be honest. The media can spot a lie a mile away. You want the media on your side, and that starts with building trust. If you do not know something, be honest. For example, "This incident just occurred, and we are working as quickly as we can to gather all of the facts and information," can be a completely honest and valid response. Keep in mind, however, that the media is going to want some information. You can keep them somewhat satisfied by setting realistic expectations. For example, "We are conducting a complete assessment now and compiling all of our information. We can provide you with a formal statement in the next hour," is an example of how to be honest but also gain a bit of time to compile your thoughts.

Having these questions in mind ahead of time can allow you to craft some potential answers.

This gives you time to proofread and refine your answers so that they convey necessary information in a way that is easy to understand. Further, it helps to have these messages created during a time when you are not under stress and not hurrying to get information out.

Once you have created your crisis-communication plan, hold "dress-rehearsal" exercises (without the children present) to ensure that everyone on your staff is on the same page. This will help you figure out what needs to be adjusted and will make your organization better prepared if an emergency does occur.

Include in your crisis-communication plan templates that can be used in the aftermath of a disaster. These templates can be drafted to cover about 80 to 90 percent of the information you would want to send after a disaster. For example, if you are in the process of evacuating, you already know your designated evacuation sites, so you can add those into your template. Likewise, you already know your plans and procedures for family reunification. You can easily plug those plans and procedures into your template. An example might be reminding parents that they need to bring a photo ID and sign out their child when they reach the evacuation site. The rest—the unknown factors, such as approximate numbers of people affected or buildings destroyed or damaged—can be left with placeholder information, allowing you to fill in the pertinent details at the time you are sending the message. The following is a brief example of a template.

Date: _____   Time: _____

Parents, as you are likely aware, today we experienced an emergency. The safety of your children is our top priority. We are currently working to gather all relevant information and to conduct a complete assessment. We understand you would like as much information as possible. Right now, we can tell you that:

[Provide a brief description of what happened. Be sure to only use details that you can confirm at this time.]

At this time, we still have a lot of unanswered questions. We are working to gather information as quickly as possible. We are also working closely with emergency officials to obtain further information and determine what additional actions may be needed. We will keep you updated and provide you with information as soon as possible. As we receive more information, we will share it via our [insert mode of communication that is working for you: social media, text messaging, email, etc.].

[You may want to include some language here asking parents not to call your program. This could be because staff are busy ensuring the safety of the children or perhaps because you had to evacuate and no one is at the program to answer the phone. Saying this helps set expectations.] We appreciate your patience as we respond to this emergency and will be back in touch with additional information as soon as possible.

––––––––––

Remember that disasters are fluid situations and require a dynamic approach. As information is constantly changing, you must also adapt your communication strategies to meet the needs of the families that you serve. This may mean changing your communication methods over time. While an initial email message to everyone may very well be appropriate, at some point the urgency will go away, and personal one-to-one phone calls between you and the families that you serve may be more appropriate. Additionally, as disaster recovery is underway, there may be increased opportunity for community participation in your rebuilding efforts, such as recruiting community volunteers to help rebuild a fence or playground or clean up your property. Just because the disaster is over does not mean that it is time to stop communicating. Your customers, clients, families, and community will want to know your status and how they can get involved and help out. As you can see, there are a lot of moving pieces in crisis communications; entire books have been written about the topic. I strongly encourage you to devote a little time to communications when conducting your emergency drills and exercises.

For additional real-world context, the online resource https://www. childhoodpreparedness.org/recovery contains numerous videos featuring real-world early childhood professionals who have experienced and recovered from disasters. Many of these videos include tips on communicating with clients and/or parents in the aftermath of a disaster.

8 Reopening Considerations

A disaster can drastically change the environment in which early childhood education programs operate. As we have learned, in some cases disasters may cause the direct and indirect releases of hazardous materials into the environment and thus make places that were at one time safe for children no longer safe. Making decisions after a disaster is difficult. Systems that are put in place and practiced before a disaster can provide considerable help in these moments. Often, the simpler a procedure is, the better, as those responsible for recovery will be dealing with numerous competing priorities. Ultimately, state or local child-care licensing regulators, in conjunction with other authorities such as the health department or fire marshal, will dictate whether early childhood programs are allowed to reopen or not.

The Choose Safe Places Programs

In 2017, the Agency for Toxic Substances and Disease Registry (ATSDR), a public health agency within the US Department of Health and Human Services, released the *Choose Safe Places for Early Care and Education (CSPECE) Guidance Manual* and began funding twenty-five cooperative agreements with states to begin building the Choose Safe Places programs. These efforts sought to be forward looking, in part by ensuring that early childhood programs were located far away from any existing environmental hazards.

Following the devastation of the 2017 hurricane season, ATSDR began the mission of creating the *Choose Safe Places for Early Care and Education: Disaster Recovery Supplement* to aid in the disaster recovery efforts for early childhood programs and facilities. In the fall of 2018, the Institute for Childhood Preparedness, acting as the lead contractor for the Region II Head Start Association, began a new project in collaboration with the National Environmental Health Association (NEHA), with disaster-recovery funding from ATSDR. The project's mission was to further support the key principles of the Choose Safe Places program and to create tools and resources that could be used in a post-disaster environment to aid recovery and minimize children's potential exposure to toxic and dangerous hazards.

One of the products from this effort was the Post-Disaster Self-Assessment Form (PDSAF). This form was developed to help child-care providers, owners, and operators assess the state of their facilities after a disaster. This new resource helped to fill a void, because no standard disaster assessment form had previously existed for early childhood programs. Designed with input from experts in early childhood, public health, environmental health, and disaster recovery, the PDSAF provides for easy identification of post-disaster hazards and considerations for early childhood programs. Ultimately, the team envisioned that this resource would be used to help clarify issues that needed attention and would inform decisions around whether it was advisable to reopen. The PDSAF was not designed to supersede any state or local authority, because often enough, the final call on whether or not a program can reopen is determined by a licensing authority. Rather, it is a resource intended to be used to create awareness and even a checklist of issues that need to be resolved before program operations can safely resume.

Like everything in a post-disaster environment, the easier something is to use, the better. The team held focus groups in Texas, Louisiana, Puerto Rico, and the USVI to receive honest feedback from early childhood professionals about the PDSAF. The form was also used in Puerto Rico in real-world conditions, after a series of earthquakes impacted the island in early 2020. The feedback gained from these efforts helped the team to further refine the form.

The information in the PDSAF provides suggestions on how to protect children from harmful environmental and chemical exposures during disaster recovery.

Using the Post-Disaster Self-Assessment Form

Parents who depend on child care need a safe place for their children to go. When early childhood programs are closed, efforts to rebuild and recover can be delayed because parents are unable to return to work. There is a palpable tension that exists between quickly restoring early childhood services and ensuring the facilities are safe for children. Often pressures come from parents on one side and from child-care regulators (fire department, public health department, and so forth) and licensing officials on the other. Unfortunately, that leaves early childhood professionals caught in the middle—as if any additional stress were needed during this time!

The Post-Disaster Self-Assessment Form is available in English and Spanish at https://www.childhood preparedness.org/recovery

The PDSAF is available in English and Spanish at https://www. childhoodpreparedness.org/recovery. Designed for ease of use, the assessment starts at the outside of the facility and gradually guides the user from outside to inside the facility. This is important, as a systematic approach is needed to ensure no hazards are missed and a thorough assessment is completed. Even though some hazards may appear obvious, it is amazing what can be overlooked if a thoughtful and consistent approach is not used.

Disasters can drastically alter landscapes and environments. For example, cracks in a foundation or basement after an earthquake may allow dangerous radon gas to enter. Fallen trees and other debris may cause the fencing around your program to be damaged or unsafe. A lack of electricity may necessitate opening windows for cooling; however, large holes in damaged window screens could allow insects to enter. These are just a few considerations of issues that you will want to examine.

As I have said before, keeping things simple is the easiest—especially during high-stress situations. When you begin to think about reopening a program, you should focus on five major areas of concern: outside, inside, food, water, and waste.

Starting Outside

When you first return to your damaged program site, be cognizant of the state of its immediate vicinity. Although your actual building may not have received heavy damage, there may be debris that would make parking or child pickup and drop off impossible. Be mindful of the different routes that parents or bus drivers would need to take to reach your building: Are all roads open and easily passable? What type of hazards would a parent, child, or staff member be presented with when attempting to enter your facility?

Before exiting your vehicle, attempt to gain as much information as you can. Be especially mindful of smells, including gas. Gas lines can be broken or damaged during disasters, especially during earthquakes. If you smell natural gas (the "rotten egg" smell of an additive to the odorless gas), get out of the area as quickly as possible.

Likewise, be alert for and very cautious of any downed power lines. Treat all power lines as if they are live and energized. If the disaster included water or rain, it is also important to ensure no power lines are touching puddles or floodwaters. The last thing you want to do is get electrocuted. If the power is out, pay attention to the placement of generators to ensure they are properly vented and not causing any potential carbon monoxide issues.

Your safety is the most important priority. If the outside area is unsafe, or you do not feel comfortable, then leave the area. These may seem like trivial things, but too often individuals will skip some of these considerations and rush into the inside of the building.

Walk around the building. Many early childhood programs are required to have fencing, and some jurisdictions are also required to have sun-shading structures. These are frequently damaged in disasters, especially in storms with high winds. Ensure the stability of these items; with weakened foundations or wind damage, they have the potential to topple over and cause injuries.

While outside, you should also check the exterior condition of windows and screens. As noted above, you may need to temporarily open windows to allow for fresh air, especially if it is hot and electricity is not available to power air-conditioning units. Also check for any obvious damage to the exterior of the building, including the roof.

Erosion of soil, displacement of insects or animals, and residue or contamination from floodwaters should also be considered while outside. Just as human beings are impacted by disasters, insects and wildlife can be as well. Depending on where you live, this might include snakes, alligators, fire ants, bears, and a myriad of other animal life that, like humans, have been displaced and are looking for new shelter or food. Keep an eye out for any usual activity that may indicate the presence of dangerous wildlife.

Moving Inside

Once inside, begin your analysis and start to take a catalog of the supplies and equipment: Are they salvageable? Are they destroyed? Are they unsafe? These are all important questions to consider. When making these determinations, it is always best to err on the side of safety. If something is questionable, throw it away. You also need to determine which items are damp or wet. Depending on the item, you may be able to wash it, dry it out, and reuse it. Dispose of bigger items, or those that do not dry easily, such as mattresses, stuffed animals, and upholstered furniture.

MOLD

Mold is a persistent challenge after disasters with water, such as floods and hurricanes. You will want to ensure that your facility and equipment is free from mold. For smaller items, mold can be cleaned following the approved process from your health department. This usually includes one cup of bleach per one gallon of water. If using bleach, be sure to follow all safety instructions and protocols, including cleaning the items in a well-ventilated area.

The photo above is from an early childhood program in Puerto Rico. The island's tropical climate, combined with the inability of staff to quickly return to the facility, led to severe mold growth. The drywall and building material had to be torn out and replaced with new material to ensure a safe environment for children.

There may be a need for extensive cleaning and restoration inside the program after the disaster. Heavy-duty cleaning processes may introduce chemicals and possibly toxic supplies into your facility. Be sure you are familiar with what supplies are being used—and do not mix chemicals. Once the cleaning has concluded, allow time for the building to be ventilated so that children are not breathing dangerous fumes. As always, store chemicals and cleaning products away from children.

WATER

We take safe and clean drinking water for granted on most days. However, disasters may damage infrastructure and make access to reliable water challenging. In some cases, water lines may burst, cutting off or diminishing the supply to your program. In other cases, sewage or other hazardous chemicals may have mixed with the fresh drinking-water supply. In either event, it is very important to recognize the vital role that water plays in the operation of your early childhood program. Importantly, we need to note here that this applies to both public and *private* drinking water sources. According to government data, more than 15 million US households receive their drinking water from private wells. These private wells are usually outside the purview of government inspections, so it is important to recognize that they require routine testing and maintenance. Natural disasters can cause contamination to private water sources, such as wells or cisterns, which may ultimately lead to a buildup of dangerous chemicals, bacteria, or other contaminants. It is strongly recommended that private wells or cisterns be inspected and tested by a professional following any natural disaster. The US Environmental Protection Agency offers a wealth of information on private water via their Private Drinking Water Wells website (https://www.epa.gov/privatewells/protect-your-homes-water).

I have seen some early childhood programs acquire bottled water after a disaster and assume that bottled water would allow them to reopen safely and resume operations. However, they quickly realize the bottled water does not come close to meeting their water needs. Think of how many times on a normal day you go to the bathroom and flush the toilet, how often you wash hands, how much water is used for cooking and cleaning. Quickly, you can begin to appreciate the large volume of water that is needed to safely run an early childhood program. Much of it is used for purposes other than drinking.

FOOD

One of the most costly items for early childhood programs is food. Because it represents a substantial portion of the budget, the reluctance to throw away food after a disaster is understandable. The good news is that not all food, especially canned food that is unexposed to external elements, must be thrown away. However, fresh food—especially items kept in the refrigerator or freezer—may need to be discarded.

If you have suffered from a prolonged loss of electricity, it is wise to dispose of your refrigerated food, especially meat, poultry, fish, and eggs. Additionally, if food stored in your freezer shows any signs of thawing, be sure to throw it away as well. Refrigerators vary greatly in their ability to keep food at safe temperatures. As noted in chapter 6, the US Food and Drug Administration says that an unopened refrigerator will keep food safe for up to four hours during a power outage (FoodSafety.gov, n.d.). Likewise, a full freezer, kept shut, will maintain a safe temperature for approximately forty-eight hours (twenty-four hours if it is only half full).

Use common sense and throw out any food that has an unusual color, odor, or appearance. When dealing with floodwater situations, including sewage backups, it is recommended that all food that has come into contact with the contaminated water be thrown away.

One last consideration concerning food is to think about dishwashing procedures. In disaster environments, it may be safer to switch to disposable plates and utensils. This will save on the amount of water needed. This may also help reduce workload, as a staff member will not be needed to wash dishes; in the aftermath of disasters, staffing may be short.

WASTE

Waste is one of those issues that is not a big deal—until it is! Ensuring you have reliable methods to get rid of sewage and garbage is very important for the safe functioning of your programs. For programs operating on private sewer or septic systems, it will be important to ensure your sewage tank has adequate space and is operating normally. If sewage disposal becomes an issue, temporary solutions, such as portable outdoor toilets, may help until normal service is restored.

Likewise, the disposal of garbage is a serious concern. For example, after its hurricanes, Puerto Rico faced a real challenge with trash and debris removal. Federally funded Head Start programs were among some of the first to hire private contractors to remove trash and other debris. Unfortunately, word of this service quickly spread, and the Head Start programs soon found their parking lots and playgrounds overrun with trash and debris from the community. Essentially, nearby residents and businesses were using Head Start as a dumping ground because they knew that a private trash collector would be removing garbage and debris. As the public trash collection service had not yet started, these were some of the only places that were receiving rubbish removal. As you can imagine, having the community bring trash and debris onto the Head Start grounds was not something that was envisioned nor wanted. It quickly became a problem, as rubbish usually also brings rodents and other undesirable pests. Eventually, the municipal trash service resumed, and the dumping stopped.

Likewise, the Florida Keys faced a massive shortage of garbage trucks coming to the small islands to remove trash. Given the lack of space to collect garbage and debris, Route 1—the only road leading into and out of the island chain—quickly turned into a dumping ground. Some piles reached upward of twenty feet high.

Wrapping Up an Assessment

An assessment is certainly a useful mechanism to help organize your thoughts and catalogue a list of damages and needed repairs. Undertaking this effort may help not only you and your program but also your regulators and/or funders. Depending on the area impacted by a disaster, those responsible for regulating early childhood programs may also be personally affected. This can lead to delays and staff shortages that can slow the regulatory agencies' ability to respond to a disaster.

While certainly not a replacement for requirements issued by your regulatory or funding agency, the PDSAF can help increase efficiency and identify the most important issues that you will need to address before reopening. By completing the self-assessment, you will be able to engage in a meaningful dialogue with the regulators and let them know precisely what your issues are. This level of organization is often helpful, as it shows a proactive approach and can help make the regulator's job easier.

While working in the Florida Keys after the hurricane, I had the opportunity to work alongside one of the regulators. I was immensely impressed by the compassion and understanding that this professional displayed. Even more impressive were the lengths she went to as she helped early childhood programs reopen in temporary spaces. Understanding that fences and shade structures had suffered extensive damage (both are a requirement in Florida), the regulator and the early childhood owners worked together to find creative solutions. Further, they worked together with community partners to help identify temporary locations where the early childhood programs could safely operate. Instead of some drawn-out process plagued by bureaucracy, the regulator actually had a portable printer in her vehicle and could—on site—print out and issue temporary operating licenses. This type of top-notch service was greatly appreciated by the community, who desperately needed a safe place to send the children so they could begin cleanup and restoration efforts. For a more detailed look at some of the issues faced by early childhood professionals in the Florida Keys after Hurricane Irma struck in September of 2017, please visit childhoodpreparedness.org/recovery and view the Florida Keys video, featuring staff from Banana Cabana Child Care.

Conclusion

Without doubt, recovery from an emergency or disaster is one of the more challenging situations that you may find yourself in. There are so many issues that require immediate attention, yet few can actually be addressed personally. Learning to pace yourself and let the process work is important. However, that is easier said than done, and feelings of despair or frustration are bound to occur. Where possible, working with trusted experts can certainly make things easier. However, even trusted experts struggle with labor and supply shortages after a disaster. We hope that reading this book and becoming more familiar with the players and processes will help you make informed decisions that are right for your center.

As I like to stress in the Preparing for the Unexpected series, the more connections you make prior to an event, the easier time you will have when disaster strikes. I strongly encourage you to take the next steps after reading this book: reach out to your insurance provider, your community organizations, your local VOAD chapter, and your local emergency management agency to better learn the resources that are available in your community.

While I certainly hope you never have to experience any disaster or emergency, I sincerely hope that, if you do, this book is helpful and can serve as a resource for you and the children you serve.

POST-HURRICANE
IMPORTANT LESSONS

"

REQUIRE
better communications systems.
There's a need for analog radios
with frequencies (this includes
amateur radios).

REMEMBER
that in addition to the children,
the staff are also experiencing
difficult situations.

**RESTRUCTURE
EMERGENCY PLANS**
and increase preparation prior to
natural disasters.

BE AWARE:
Child-care centers need to know if
they are in close proximity to
dangerous places or helpful
resources—this includes where
they are planning to relocate
in case of disaster.

 Centers
**NEED GENERATORS
AND WAREHOUSES**
full of materials and supplies.

HAVE A MAP
of safe places to go,
and know in advance where
resources are available.

Have
BETTER SECURITY
so centers
don't get vandalized.

ANTICIPATE
the community using the
child-care facilities as a dumping
ground for trash and debris,
and recognize all of the hazards
this brings with it.

 STOCK UP
on supplies and first-aid kits in
advance of another hurricane.

"

Appendix: Online Resources

Adventist Community Services:
https://www.communityservices.org/our-ministry/disaster-response

American Red Cross:
https://www.redcross.org/about-us/our-work/disaster-relief.html

Catholic Charities USA:
https://www.catholiccharitiesusa.org/our-vision-and-ministry/disaster-relief/

Evangelical Lutheran Church of America:
https://www.elca.org/Our-Work/Relief-and-Development/Lutheran-Disaster-Response/How-We-Work

Institute for Childhood Preparedness:
https://www.childhoodpreparedness.org/recovery

National Insurance Crime Bureau:
https://www.nicb.org/reportfraud

National Child Traumatic Stress Network:
https://www.nctsn.org/sites/default/files/resources/fact-sheet/secondary_traumatic_stress_child_serving_professionals.pdf

National Voluntary Organizations Active in Disaster:
https://www.nvoad.org/about-us/

Save the Children:
https://www.savethechildren.org/

References and Recommended Reading

3R's Construction. n.d. "How Does an Earthquake Affect Radon Levels?" 3R's Construction. https://www.3rsconstruction.com/home-remediation/earthquake-radon-levels/

Adams, Richard E., Joseph A. Boscarino, and Charles R. Figley. 2006. "Compassion Fatigue and Psychological Distress among Social Workers: A Validation Study." *American Journal of Orthopsychiatry* 76(1): 103–108.

Afshar, Majid, Mahesh Ranu, David Ansell, and Thomas Bleck. 2011. "Narrative Review: Tetanus—A Health Threat after Natural Disasters in Developing Countries." *Annals of Internal Medicine* 154(5): 329–335.

Agency for Toxic Substances and Disease Registry. 2017. *Choose Safe Places for Early Care and Education (CSPECE) Guidance Manual.* Washington, DC: US Department of Health and Human Services and Atlanta, GA: Centers for Disease Control and Prevention. https://www.atsdr.cdc.gov/safeplacesforECE/docs/Choose_Safe_Places_508_final.pdf

Agency for Toxic Substances and Disease Registry. 2020. *Choose Safe Places for Early Care and Education: Disaster Recovery Supplement.* Washington, DC: US Department of Health and Human Services and Atlanta, GA: Centers for Disease Control and Prevention. https://www.atsdr.cdc.gov/safeplacesforece/docs/disaster_recovery_supplement-508.pdf

Alaska Division of Geological and Geophysical Surveys. n.d. "Radon Testing after Earthquakes." Fairbanks, AK: Alaska Division of Geological and Geophysical Surveys. https://dggs.alaska.gov/webpubs/dggs/ic/text/ic083.pdf

Boulet-Desbareau, Pierre. 2013. "Unsolicited In-Kind Donations & Other Inappropriate Humanitarian Goods: Strategic Plan." Geneva, Switzerland: United Nations Office for the Coordination of Humanitarian Affairs. https://emergency-log.weebly.com/uploads/2/5/2/4/25246358/ubd_report_eng_-_final_for_printing_2.pdf

California Earthquake Authority. 2022. "Protect Your Home from Earthquake Damage." CEA. https://www.earthquakeauthority.com/

Campbell, Richard. 2017. *Structure Fires in Educational Properties.* Quincy, MA: National Fire Protection Association. https://www.nfpa.org/-/media/Files/News-and-Research/Fire-statistics-and-reports/Building-and-life-safety/oseducation.pdf

Center for International Disaster Information, United States Agency for International Development (USAID). n.d. Donations Calculator. https://www.cidi.org/how-to-help/donations-calculator/

Centers for Disease Control and Prevention. 2014. *Crisis Emergency Risk Communication.* Atlanta, GA: Centers for Disease Control and Prevention. https://emergency.cdc.gov/cerc/ppt/cerc_2014edition_Copy.pdf

Centers for Disease Control and Prevention. 2017. "Preventing Carbon Monoxide Poisoning after a Disaster." Centers for Disease Control and Prevention. https://www.cdc.gov/disasters/cofacts.html

Centers for Disease Control and Prevention. 2019. "Adverse Childhood Experiences (ACEs): Preventing Early Trauma to Improve Adult Health." Centers for Disease Control and Prevention. https://www.cdc.gov/vitalsigns/aces/index.html

Centers for Disease Control and Prevention. 2020. "Tdap/Td Vaccines: Addressing Common Questions about Tdap/Td Vaccination for Adults." Atlanta, GA: Centers for Disease Control and Prevention. https://www.cdc.gov/vaccines/hcp/adults/downloads/fs-tdap-hcp.pdf

Centers for Disease Control and Prevention. 2021a. "Data and Statistics on Children's Mental Health." Centers for Disease Control and Prevention. https://www.cdc.gov/childrensmentalhealth/data.html

Centers for Disease Control and Prevention. 2021b. "Personal Hygiene during an Emergency." Centers for Disease Control and Prevention. https://www.cdc.gov/healthywater/emergency/hygiene-handwashing-diapering/handwashing-and-hygiene-during-emergencies.html

Centers for Disease Control and Prevention. 2021c. "Making Water Safe in an Emergency." CDC. https://www.cdc.gov/healthywater/emergency/making-water-safe.html

Chavez, Nicole. 2017. "Hurricane Maria: Puerto Rico Officials Describe 'Apocalyptic' Conditions." Sept. 24. CNN. https://www.cnn.com/2017/09/24/americas/hurricane-maria-puerto-rico-aftermath/index.html

Committee for Economic Development of the Conference Board. 2019. *Child Care in State Economies: 2019 Update.* Arlington, VA: CED. https://www.ced.org/assets/reports/childcareimpact/181104%20CCSE%20Report%20Jan30.pdf

Committee on Homeland Security Hearing. 2005. *Homeland Security Hearing on Ensuring Operability during Catastrophic Events Before the Subcommittee on Emergency Preparedness, Science, and Technology*, 109th Congress (Oct. 26). Written statement of Dr. Peter M. Fonash, Deputy Manager, National Communications System, DHS.

Community Foundation of the Virgin Islands. 2018. *U.S. Virgin Islands Kids Count Data Book 2016: Our Children in Focus*. St. Thomas, USVI: Community Foundation of the Virgin Islands. https://cfvi.net/wp-content/uploads/2019/02/2016-Data-Book.pdf

Community Partnership of the Ozarks. n.d. *Don't Let One Disaster Lead to Another: Disaster Toolkit*. Springfield, MO: Community Partnership of the Ozarks. https://mdem.maryland.gov/Documents/Local%20Recovery%20Planning%20Support%20Toolkit/Long%20Term%20Recovery%20Committee%20Guide%20and%20Resources/Case%20Studies/Joplin,%20MO%20Case%20Study%20Information%20and%20Materials/Responding%20to%20a%20Disaster%20A%20Prevention%20Toolkit%20(Joplin).pdf

Cox Marrero, Anitza María, et al. 2018a. *Impact of Hurricane Maria on Puerto Rico's Children, Vol. 1*. Instituto Desarrollo Juventud. https://assets-global.website-files.com/60f311e9e2e57d523d28bba2/6162279d7b8725064060c7a1_35.pdf

Cox, Marrero, Anitza Maria, et al. 2018b. "The Impact of Hurricane Maria on Children in Puerto Rico." Instituto Desarollo Juventud. Slide presentation. https://issuu.com/coleccionpuertorriquena/docs/instituto_juventud

De Bellis, Michael D., and Abigail Zisk. 2014. "The Biological Effects of Childhood Trauma." *Child and Adolescent Psychiatric Clinics of North America* 23(2): 185–222.

Ericson, Matthew, Archie Tse, and Jodi Wilgoren. 2005. "Katrina's Diaspora." *New York Times*, October 2, 2005. https://archive.nytimes.com/www.nytimes.com/imagepages/2005/10/02/national/nationalspecial/20051002diaspora_graphic.html

Federal Emergency Management Agency. 1996. *Guide for All-Hazard Emergency Operations Planning*. Washington, D.C.: Federal Emergency Planning Agency. https://www.fema.gov/pdf/plan/slg101.pdf

Federal Emergency Management Agency. 2021. "Earthquake Insurance." FEMA. https://www.fema.gov/emergency-managers/risk-management/earthquake/insurance

Foodsafety.gov. n.d. "Food Safety During Power Outage: Refrigerated Food and Power Outages: When to Save It and When to Throw It Out." Foodsafety.gov. https://www.foodsafety.gov/food-safety-charts/food-safety-during-power-outage#refrigerated

Gammon, Katharine. 2012. "Sex Toys, Winter Coats, and Spanish Flags: The Uselessness of Post-Disaster Donations." Fast Company. https://www.fastcompany.com/2679177/sex-toys-winter-coats-and-spanish-flags-the-uselessness-of-post-disaster-donations

Garrett, Amy, et al. 2019. "Longitudinal Changes in Brain Function Associated with Symptom Improvement in Youth with PTSD." *Journal of Psychiatric Research* 114: 161–169.

Glynn, Sarah Jane, and Danielle Corley. 2016. "The Cost of Work-Family Policy Inaction: Quantifying the Costs Families Currently Face as a Result of Lacking U.S. Work-Family Policies." Center for American Progress. https://www.americanprogress.org/issues/women/reports/2016/09/22/143877/the-cost-of-inaction/

Grace, Molly. 2022. "Earthquake Insurance: What Does It Cost and Is It Worth It?" Rocket Mortgage. https://www.rocketmortgage.com/learn/earthquake-insurance

Harbour, Sarita. 2021. "7 Home Insurance Claims and How You Can Avoid Them." The Hartford. https://extramile.thehartford.com/home/home-insurance/avoid-common-claims/

Hartwig, Robert P., and Claire Wilkinson. 2010. *Hurricane Katrina: The Five Year Anniversary.* New York: Insurance Information Institute. https://www.iii.org/sites/default/files/1007Katrina5Anniversary.pdf

Herzog, Dale. 2018. "Ever Sent Clothes, Supplies or Toys in Response to a Disaster? Here's What Probably Happened to It." Ideas.TED.com. https://ideas.ted.com/after-a-disaster-dont-send-toys-or-clothing-send-money-heres-why/

Holguín-Veras, José, et al. 2014. "Material Convergence: An Important and Understudied Disaster Phenomenon." *Natural Hazards Review* 15(1): 1–12.

Insurance Information Institute. 2017. "U.S. Homeowners Give Record High Satisfaction Scores To Their Insurers." Insurance Information Institute. https://www.iii.org/press-release/us-homeowners-give-record-high-satisfaction-scores-to-their-insurers-031317

Insurance Information Institute. 2022. "Facts + Statistics: Homeowners and Renters Insurance." Insurance Information Institute. https://www.iii.org/fact-statistic/facts-statistics-homeowners-and-renters-insurance

Iqbal, Shahed, et al. 2012. "A Review of Disaster-Related Carbon Monoxide Poisoning: Surveillance, Epidemiology, and Opportunities for Prevention." *American Journal of Public Health* 102(10): 1957–1963.

Leser, Kendall A., Julie Looper-Coats, and Andrew R. Roszak. 2019. "Emergency Preparedness Plans and Perceptions Among a Sample of United States Childcare Providers." *Disaster Medicine and Public Health Preparedness* 13(4): 704–708.

Maslow, Abraham. 1943. "A Theory of Human Motivation." *Psychological Review* 50(4): 370–396.

May Recreation. 2021. "Inspecting Your Playground After a Flood." May Recreation. https://info.mayrecreation.com/blog/inspecting-your-playground-after-a-flood

Michael, Noreen, et al. 2019. *Community Needs Assessment: Understanding the Needs of Vulnerable Children and Families in the US Virgin Islands Post Hurricanes Irma and Maria.* St. Thomas, USVI: Caribbean Exploratory Research Center, School of Nursing, University of the Virgin Islands. https://www.uvi.edu/academics/nursing/cerc/CFVI-CERC%20Community%20Needs%20Assessment%20E-Report_February%202019.pdf

Morgan, Josh. 2021. "Cobb County Firefighters Evacuate Kids at Daycare Due to Flooding." CBS46 News. https://www.cbs46.com/news/cobb-county-firefighters-evacuate-kids-at-daycare-due-to-flooding/article_ff1b3c58-012f-11ec-b61e-6b2ce661c6ea.html

Morris, Frank. 2011. "For Joplin's Children, Tornado's Effects Persist." *Morning Edition,* September 15. National Public Radio. https://www.npr.org/2011/09/15/140476898/for-joplins-children-tornados-effects-persist

National Association for the Education of Young Children. 2018. "11 Tips for Helping Children Who Have Experienced Disaster." *Teaching Young Children* 11(3). https://www.naeyc.org/system/files/11tips_11.3.pdf

National Association of Insurance Commissioners. 2021. "Hurricane Deductibles." NAIC. https://content.naic.org/cipr_topics/topic_hurricane_deductibles.htm

National Center for Disaster Preparedness and Children's Health Fund. 2010. *Legacy of Katrina: The Impact of a Flawed Recovery on Vulnerable Children of the Gulf Coast.* New York, NY: Columbia University Libraries Academic Commons, Columbia University. https://academiccommons.columbia.edu/doi/10.7916/D8H420TK

National Hurricane Center and Central Pacific Hurricane Center. n.d. "Hurricanes in History." National Hurricane Center and Central Pacific Hurricane Center. https://www.nhc.noaa.gov/outreach/history/

National Oceanic and Atmospheric Administration, National Severe Storms Laboratory. n.d. "Severe Weather 101: Flood Basics." NSSL. https://www.nssl.noaa.gov/education/svrwx101/floods/

National Resource Center for Health and Safety in Child Care and Early Education. 2020. "Chapter 5: Facilities, Supplies, Equipment, and Environmental Health: 5.6.0.1. First Aid and Emergency Supplies." Caring for Our Children. https://nrckids.org/CFOC/Database/5.6.0.1

National Scientific Council on the Developing Brain. 2014. *Excessive Stress Disrupts the Architecture of the Developing Brain*. Working paper no. 3. Cambridge, MA: Center on the Developing Child, Harvard University. https://46y5eh11fhgw3ve3ytpwxt9r-wpengine.netdna-ssl.com/wp-content/uploads/2005/05/Stress_Disrupts_Architecture_Developing_Brain-1.pdf

National Weather Service. n.d.a. "The 1993 'Storm of the Century.'" National Weather Service. https://www.weather.gov/tbw/93storm

National Weather Service. n.d.b. "Hurricane Sandy, October 29, 2012." National Weather Service. https://www.weather.gov/okx/HurricaneSandy5Year

NC Division of Social Services and the Family and Children's Resource Program. 2012. "How Trauma Affects Child Brain Development." *Practice Notes* 17(2). https://practicenotes.org/v17n2/brain.htm

Reckdahl, Katy. 2015. "The Lost Children of Katrina." *The Atlantic*. https://www.theatlantic.com/education/archive/2015/04/the-lost-children-of-katrina/389345/

Region II Head Start Association. 2019. "Update: Puerto Rico Disaster Recovery." Region II Head Start Association. https://www.region2headstart.org/post/puerto-rico-disaster-recovery

Rudolph, Shari. n.d. "Avoiding the Second Disaster: How (Not) to Donate During a Crisis." Good360. https://good360.org/blog-posts/avoiding-the-second-disaster-how-not-to-donate-during-a-crisis/

Scott, Michon. 2018. "Hurricane Maria's Devastation of Puerto Rico." NOAA. Climate.gov. https://www.climate.gov/news-features/understanding-climate/hurricane-marias-devastation-puerto-rico

Sheperd, Cristin. 2017. "After a Flood, Inspect Playgrounds from the Ground Up." Noah's Park and Playgrounds. https://noahsplay.com/blog/noahsplayafter-a-flood-inspect-playgrounds-from-the-ground-up-/

Sprang, Ginny, and Leslie Anne Ross. 2011. "Secondary Traumatic Stress: A Fact Sheet for Child-Serving Professionals." Los Angeles, CA, and Durham, NC: National Child Traumatic Stress Network. https://www.nctsn.org/sites/default/files/resources/fact-sheet/secondary_traumatic_stress_child_serving_professionals.pdf

Stevens, Katharine B. 2017. *Workforce of Today, Workforce of Tomorrow: The Business Case for High-Quality Childcare*. Washington, DC: US Chamber of Commerce. https://www.uschamberfoundation.org/sites/default/files/Workforce%20of%20Today%20Workforce%20of%20Tomorrow%20Report.pdf

Substance Abuse and Mental Health Services Administration. n.d. *Tips for Talking to Children and Youth After Traumatic Events: A Guide for Parents and Educators*. Rockville, MD: SAMHSA. https://www.samhsa.gov/sites/default/files/tips-talking-to-children-after-traumatic-event.pdf

Substance Abuse and Mental Health Services Administration. 2018. *Behavioral Health Conditions in Children and Youth Exposed to Natural Disasters*. Supplemental Research Bulletin. Rockville, MD: SAMHSA. https://www.samhsa.gov/sites/default/files/srb-childrenyouth-8-22-18.pdf

US Department of Health and Human Services. 2005. "Surgeon General Releases National Health Advisory on Radon." Press release, January 13. HHS Press Office. http://www.adph.org/radon/assets/surgeon_general_radon.pdf

US Department of Homeland Security, Earthquake Country Alliance, and Federal Alliance for Safe Homes. n.d. *Ready Business Quakesmart Toolkit*. Washington, DC: Federal Alliance for Safe Homes. https://www.ready.gov/sites/default/files/2020-04/ready-buisness_quakesmart_toolkit.pdf

US Environmental Protection Agency. n.d. *The National Radon Action Plan: A Strategy for Saving Lives*. Washington, DC: Environmental Protection Agency. https://www.epa.gov/sites/default/files/2019-05/documents/nrap-a_strategy_for_saving_lives_-_final.pdf

US Federal Emergency Management Agency and Federal Alliance for Safe Homes. n.d.a. *Ready Business How-To Guide*. Washington, DC: Federal Alliance for Safe Homes. https://www.ready.gov/sites/default/files/2020-04/ready_business_how-to-guide.pdf

US Federal Emergency Management Agency and Federal Alliance for Safe Homes. n.d.b. *Ready Business Power Outage Toolkit*. Washington, DC: Federal Alliance for Safe Homes. https://www.ready.gov/sites/default/files/2020-04/ready_business_power-outage-toolkit.pdf

US Virgin Islands Department of Health. 2020. *United States Virgin Islands Community Health Assessment*. Christiansted, USVI: USVI Department of Health. https://doh.vi.gov/sites/default/files/USVI_CHA%202020_Final_06.02.20.pdf

Vargas, Ramon Antonio. 2021. "Frightening Surge in Carbon Monoxide Poisonings after Hurricane Ida: Generators 'Can Kill.'" Nola.com. https://www.nola.com/news/hurricane/article_cd8ec726-0b4e-11ec-b63c-1f17f06eee67.html

WWL Staff. 2021. "Death Toll Registers at 10 Total for Hurricane Ida after Man Dies from CO Poisoning." 4WWL. https://www.wwltv.com/article/weather/hurricane/death-toll-registers-at-10-total-for-hurricane-ida/289-56714f9f-7e62-4a37-ab4e-33c6cb839580

Index